We Can
Keep Them in the
Church

Other books by Gary L. Hopkins

It Takes a Church

We Can Keep Them in the Church

Success stories and ideas that really work

How to love our children so they won't leave

Compiled by Myrna Tetz with Gary L. Hopkins

Pacific Press® Publishing Association
Nampa, Idaho
Oshawa, Ontario, Canada
www.pacificpress.com

Designed by Michelle C. Petz
Cover photo © Digital Vision / Getty Images

Additional copies of this book are available by calling toll free 1-800-765-6955
or visiting http://www.adventistbookcenter.com

Scripture references marked NEB are from *The New English Bible,* copyright © by the Delegates of the Oxford
University Press and the Syndics of the Cambridge University Press, 1961, 1970. Used by permission.
Scripture references marked NIV are from the Holy Bible, New International Version, copyright © 1973, 1978,
1984 by the International Bible Society. Used by permission of Zondervan Bible Publishers.
Scripture references marked NASB are from the *New American Standard Bible,* © The Lockman Foundation
1960, 1962, 1963, 1968, 1971, 1972, 1973, 1975, 1977. Used by permission.
Scripture references marked NKJV are from the New King James Version. Copyright © 1973, 1978, 1984 by
International Bible Society. Used by permission of Zondervan Bible Publishers.

Library of Congress Cataloging-in-Publication data:

We can keep them in the church : how to love our children so they won't leave :
sucess stories that really work / compiled by Myrna Tetz with Gary Hopkins.
p.cm
ISBN: 0-8163-1998-7
1. Seventh-day Adventists—Membership. 2. Church with youth—Seventh-day Adventists 3. Church work
with children—Seventh-day Adventists. I. Tetz, Myrna, 1934- II. Hopkins, Gary, 1948-

BX5154.W39 2004
259'.2—dc22   2003058095

04 05 06 07 08 • 5 4 3 2 1

Dedication

This book is dedicated to the memory of my mother, Harriet Peterson Johnson, who all her life lovingly cared for children and young people. She taught Kindergarten Sabbath School, played games with the young, and created fun things for children to do whenever adults dominated a gathering.

There are thousands of others who have loved and who love children selflessly as she did. I'm gratefully including them in this dedication as well. In ways we may not realize, her goals and dreams live on. Her death is not final; she is too much a part of those who knew her.

— *Myrna Tetz*

Preface

My husband and I were visiting a Bible study group, and after the discussion the leader asked what we're doing now that we are both retired. Bob explained his part-time ministry and then, pointing at me, said that I was putting together a book. I said that, as a church, we are losing nearly half our young people, that I believed we could keep our youth, and that I had asked a variety of individuals to write about how this could happen. Heads nodded and people agreed that something needed to happen. Then someone asked, "Why do we want our young people to stay in the church?"

I was stunned. Inside my head I was saying, "Why *wouldn't* we want to keep our children in the church?" Did the person who asked that question think the possibility of our young people meeting Christ in our church was minimal? Other questions arose, so this one wasn't answered, but afterwards I thought about it a lot. The question is a good one. Why *do* we want our youth to stay in the church?

Of course, there are obvious answers: We desire them to live Christian lives exempt from the evils that surround them. We're anxious that they minister to those who are hungry, both physically and spiritually. We want them to be saved when Jesus comes. So, yes, we want them to stay as active, loyal, dedicated, converted members of the Seventh-day Adventist Church.

And if they choose to leave, what would we want them to say? That they hated the church? That they were not loved? That the people in the church, particularly the older ones, didn't care if they were there or not?

Suppose your son or your daughter or your friends' children or your pastor's offspring were to choose another lifestyle. Wouldn't you want them to be able to say, "Oh, let me tell you, the Seventh-day Adventist church I attended was a warm and friendly place. Even though I made noise during the services, dressed inappropriately at times, wore a ring in my nose and one in my belly button that could be seen, acted like I didn't care, and sang music they didn't like, I was definitely loved. There were adults there besides my parents who spoke to me and hugged me every time they saw me when I was a child and during my rebellious teenage years. And they still keep in touch by phone, by letter, and by very meaningful gifts. Sometimes they even invite me to their homes, feed me, and ask what I'm doing and *how* I'm doing. I certainly was and still am loved. I have such fond memories of attending the Seventh-day Adventist church."

Does this description fit your church?

How This Book Came to Be

Two events piqued my interest in the question "What could we do to keep our young people?": a presentation by Jose Rojas on youth music groups and our reactions to them and Willie Oliver's story about a man whose children were finding church boring (see the Rojas and Oliver interviews in this book). I put some scrambled thoughts down in an email to Gary Hopkins describing my new obsession and asking if he thought the topic was worth pursuing. (I didn't know about his book *It Takes a Church,* which was just being released at the time.) Within a few minutes (typical Hopkins!) he sent an email saying that he had called Tim Lale, book acquisition editor at Pacific Press and told him about this proposed book. Almost immediately the telephone rang; Tim was on the line encouraging us to carry on.

Prospective authors—including church leaders, children's and youth ministries directors, young pastors, and members—were contacted, deadlines were set, and almost all of those who were encouraged to write accepted, with no payment promised. As the manuscripts came in, I became excited: If every Seventh-day Adventist would read this book and put into practice what these individuals have suggested, our children and young people would become vibrant, happy, enthusiastic members of our church. And what's more, they'd stay.

I invite you to read this book, internalize the suggestions, and pray about our church and our ministry to children and young people. Then do your best to change *your* church into a loving, happy, accepting group of dedicated members—if it isn't already, that is!

—Myrna Tetz

Space limitations kept a lot of good stuff—like the whole story of Estera Stefanovich (see Appendix C)—out of this book. To see this extra material, look up www.adventistbookcenter.com/olink.tpl?sku=0816319987.

Table of Contents

Introduction

by Tim Lale

Some people in the Seventh-day Adventist Church feel dissatisfied with the status quo. I am one of them, and I suspect you are too. We wish to see change, but we're not sure exactly how the church should change or who could make it happen. The purpose of this book is to assemble a faint picture of what you might see going on at your church if it were full of happy, committed church members *of all ages.*

What we don't need is more bad news. We already know that about half of the young people raised in the church leave it when they reach adulthood. We know that the membership of the North American church is static in many areas. We know that the divorce rate of American Seventh-day Adventists is virtually indistinguishable from that of the U.S. population as a whole. We know that enrollments in Seventh-day Adventist Church schools have declined steeply in the past twenty years. If you want woeful facts about the state of the church, you can find plenty.

What if we agreed that the future for our young people could be a lot better? What if we decided to change our basic assumptions and started down a different path?

If the idea of change seems dangerous, let me assure you that there are no theological innovations in this book, only a bunch of loud affirmations. This is not a book about worship style or church-growth models or other subjects we argue about. This is a book of stories about how to form the most positive, happy, Christlike assumptions about ourselves and each other and then pass them to the younger generations. It is filled with anecdotes of individuals who have found ways to draw fellow believers, especially the younger ones, into church fellowship and relationship with God. Individuals from all the ministries of our church—lay members and leaders—have contributed their stories and their vision, and I'm excited about the contribution each has made. You will like this book if you like good news. You will enjoy it and relate to it if you want good things to happen in your church from now on.

What's the formula for happy church members, young and old? It actually comes from the prequel to this book, another book called *It Takes a Church*. In it, Gary Hopkins and Joyce Hopp share this radical observation: *The way to keep young people in the Seventh-day Adventist Church is to surround them with adults who acknowledge them by name, display a loving, caring attitude toward them, and show concern for them and help them whenever possible.* This formula, when applied, has done some radically positive things for children and teens.

Kids with supportive adults in their lives are much more likely to choose to *avoid destructive behaviors* like smoking and premarital sex than are other young people, regardless of whether the supportive adults have ever mentioned these subjects by name. The adults in a church don't have to tell the kids what to do; they only have to be loving and supportive. Why? Because young people already have lots of information, and they have already been told many times what is the right thing to do. What they may not have had is a sense that they are *important to the adults in their lives*. The sense that we care is the single biggest gift we can give them—and the surest way to keep them in the church. Children and youth who have this gift make good decisions in the tough situations of life and may not even realize why. And these kids will come back to church looking for more good news and support.

Of course, parents are the most important adults in the life of a young person. For many children, their parents' level of love and care and involvement is the biggest predictor of whether or not they grow into relationship with God and the church. The model of faith they receive at home is the most influential one in the child's life. Let's acknowledge, however, that some of the best Christian parents around have produced children who turned away from God and the church when they grew up. Only God Himself knows what is in the minds of these children. He gave the choice of belief or unbelief to every single one of His human creations, and that means there are no guarantees. We are not looking for a formula that deprives children of the choice to serve Him out of love.

But parents are not meant to carry the burden of their children's spiritual formation alone. Just as we need the members of the church, the body of Christ, for our own spiritual strength, so parents need the church congregation as a contributor to the spiritual growth of their children. That's where the rest of us come in. Do we need to become experts at something or take all kinds of training? No. As we learn ways of showing care and love to children and young people who enter our circle, we help to lift them up out of the muck of the world and draw them to the warmth and light of God's love. And the question of whether or not they stay in the church takes care of itself.

Whenever I hear someone say, "We are losing our young people," I shudder. It suggests that somehow we own them, that somehow we are losing what, as a church, is ours. I believe that is false. As I said earlier, there are no guarantees concerning the young people connected with the church because God has given each of us the right to choose. But every week there are opportunities to help children and youth understand how important they are. From the Bible and the stories of others we can learn how to help them be saved, and there are ways we can remove every barrier that might prevent it from happening.

However, the main reason the words "We are losing our young people" bothers me is that it covers up what has really happened until now. I believe that teens and young adults have left the church mainly because we, the adults in church, didn't connect with them when we had the opportunity—not out of malice or intentional slight, maybe, but because it is not our habit, very often, to seek them out in simple ways. I don't say this to create a sense of guilt. Feelings of guilt don't help us progress. This is just recognition of a root problem. And it is the source of the solution.

Is this a challenge that you can't see a way to meet? From the human point of view it may seem that way. Many of us feel we don't have much of anything to give to a child or teen. How do we make ourselves care more if we already care? How can we find something inside us that we haven't felt before?

Again, I think the answer is simple but overlooked. God's love is available to us in quantities that we would actually buckle under if we asked for a lot more consciousness of it. Throughout the Bible God says, "Call on Me. Ask Me for stuff. Don't hold back. Prove Me now." He says over and over, "When you know what it feels like to be loved this much, you'll be bursting with it. You'll have to share it—to pass it on because you won't be able to keep it in."

Sometimes I have a little bit of a sense of how much God loves me. It's like an amazing warmth—an out-of-this-world sense of security; a wonderful feeling that I am very valuable and esteemed and cared about. I want to know more about it and feel it more, and I want to be able to pass it on to the children in my family and my church.

So, do we start this process of change with a firm resolve to do things differently? No, that's not the first step. We don't make it happen with our own determination. We simply go to God and say in prayer as often as we can, "Please fill us up and make us know Your love. Please change us so that we can't help caring about every child and teenager and young adult we meet. Please make us impulsively kind and interested and loving. Please help us to change kids by turning their hearts to You." And then we leave it to Him to grow our hearts.

Is the world full of temptations for children and youth? Yes.

Is it saturated with images, objects, ideas, and attitudes that run counter to God's culture? Of course it is.

Is it possible to insulate young people against this stinking mess without completely and totally sheltering them from it? I believe it is!

Is it possible to help the majority of our kids accept the commandments of God and the faith of Jesus as their own? With a God-given change in *our* attitude and habits, it seems very possible.

Is it possible to have too many young people in a church? I don't think so—but let's try to find out!

More Than a Message

by Gary Hopkins

Gary Hopkins is Assistant Professor of Health Promotion and Education at the School of Public Health, Loma Linda University, and Director of the Center for Prevention Research at the Institute for Prevention of Addictions at Andrews University. This chapter is adapted from an article by the same name published in the Adventist Review, *March 6, 2003, pp. 26-30. Used by permission.*

Sharon is a young woman who works for an insurance firm in Kansas City. She is single and loves life. She's bright, fun, popular, and full of energy.

Sharon was raised in a Seventh-day Adventist home to loving parents. Her mother works as an assistant manager of a large department store and her father as the pastor of a large Adventist church. During her early years Sharon always attended church. She loved learning her memory verses. When she was young she would stand up in front of church and recite flawlessly all thirteen memory verses from the quarter.

Sharon attended Adventist schools from the first grade through college. She took all the required Bible courses and attended vespers and Sabbath afternoon spiritual meetings as scheduled by her father's church and her schools. In high school she sang in the choir, played the flute in the band, and worked at the church camp each summer.

While in college Sharon began attending worship services and other church activities less frequently. If you asked her why, she would have had a difficult time explaining the reasons. But she clearly felt less interested in the church and spiritual matters and felt somewhat guilty for her lack of interest.

Since finishing college, Sharon goes to church only when she's with her parents. Other than that, the church is a part of her past and has nothing to do with her present life. Sharon isn't an alcoholic, but she does drink on occasion, though never to drunkenness. She doesn't take drugs but is sexually intimate with her boyfriend.

Sharon knows the message of Jesus, the doctrine of salvation, the 2,300-day prophecy, Daniel and Revelation, the parables, and more. She understands the meaning of the Sabbath and is certain that there will be a second coming of Christ and a final judgment. She knows the message. She knows it well. Because Sharon does not practice what she knows to be true, we might think that what she needs is a better understanding of the message. Nothing could be further from the truth. Sharon's situation, a very common one, needs to be examined from a different perspective.

Why Do They Leave?

If you look around and maybe at yourself, you might find people like Sharon. She also knows that she should exercise routinely but doesn't. Does that sound like you? Sharon has many friends who know well that smoking is dangerous and shortens life, yet who smoke. Does that sound like people you know? Sharon knows being overweight can lead to less than optimal outcomes, but finds herself a little heavy. Sound like you? In many regards, Sharon *knows,* but her knowing doesn't necessarily translate into doing—just as her understanding of the biblical message has not translated into her applying that message to her life.

If you look at our church today, it's easy to see that maybe half or more of our young people are leaving the church when they finish high school. People commonly conclude that we aren't preaching the message of the Bible well enough. I disagree. The kids who are leaving the church are leaving with a pretty good understanding of the church's message. Dr. Bailey Gillespie, the lead researcher in the Valuegenesis studies, tells me that by the sixth grade our kids generally understand the story of Jesus, the good news of the forgiveness of sin, the second coming of Christ, the Sabbath, and other basic spiritual matters. Our kids are leaving for other reasons.

Over the past few years several colleagues of mine and I have been studying what we can do to prevent the behaviors that are well known to contribute to the transmission of HIV, the virus that causes AIDS. We've focused our work on adolescents between the ages of twelve and twenty or so. We're studying young people because globally, more than 50 percent of the new cases of AIDS are found in those less than twenty-five years of age.

As a part of our research we ask questions that test the participants' AIDS knowledge. Using a written questionnaire, we ask the young people—usually students enrolled in high school—if they can get AIDS from toilet seats, mosquitoes, holding hands, and so forth. During the analysis phase we actually score the students' proficiency in the AIDS knowledge section.

In research conducted on samples in Romania, the Philippines, the Caribbean, Armenia, the United States, Canada, and other locations, we've learned that generally students are well educated regarding HIV/AIDS. They tend to know the information that they need to know.

Our questionnaire also measures the extent to which participants have engaged in sexual intercourse and drug use—both behaviors known to be associated with the transmission of the AIDS virus. Our findings vary, but one item keeps emerging in every study: There tends to be virtually no association between their AIDS knowledge and their behavior. In other words, regardless of how much they know about AIDS, they tend to practice behaviors that put them at risk—sometimes very high risk—for contracting or transmitting the AIDS virus. It doesn't appear that AIDS education alone will result in effective prevention of AIDS.

First Corinthians 13 makes a point that I believe directs itself to this situation. It says that we have to love people. It makes this point very clearly. Our kids aren't leaving because they don't understand the message; they are leaving because our churches have become *message only* organizations. We assume that we have the gospel. Well, unless your church is a caring, extremely loving organization, then it clearly doesn't have the gospel. Part of the message is information, but there's another part—love. You can't separate the two. Message alone isn't working to keep our kids or even the results of our evangelism and it never will.

After puzzling about this very weak relationship between what we know and what we do, I searched for something that I already knew but apparently only poorly understood. First and foremost it is our responsibility to love. The Bible is replete with instructions to love our brother. It says the most important commandments are to love God and then to love our fellow human beings. First Corinthians 13 makes this very clear: If we speak in all tongues but don't love, we are no more than a clanging cymbal. If we have the faith to move mountains and don't love, it's not worth anything. If we gave all that we have and don't love, we are wasting our time.

So, I can't help but wonder if our church hasn't turned into an information-only organization. Now, I absolutely believe in the accuracy of the Adventist message. But if all we have is a message, we clearly don't have enough. To clarify, in the absence of love, our message appears to be insufficient. We must move beyond the message alone and become a loving organization. And I believe that we need to learn how to do this by starting with our kids.

Is your church absolutely and completely oriented to the spiritual development of your kids? Or does your nominating committee have to get on their knees to beg adults to work in the children's and youth's Sabbath School departments? I think that if someone ran into your adult Sabbath School class this coming Sabbath and screamed, "There's a fire in the kids' divisions!" most of you would get up and run to help without any hesitation at all. Well, there *is* an emergency in those divisions. Many or most of those kids will leave this church, and many will stray away from a relationship with Jesus Christ.

We may try to correct this crisis by bringing in great speakers with a wonderful message, purchasing well-made videos that seem extremely convincing, or maybe purchasing loud sound equipment so that the kids can play their own variety of music. But the issue here isn't a lack of knowing what the speakers or videos have to say or the absence of music with a beat, it's a lack of caring. Do you get it? The problem isn't the kids; it's you and me. We don't care enough for the kids of our church to devote our churches to their welfare. Most churches are about adults and about message.

How Do We Learn to Love?

So, how do we learn to love? Maybe this is told best in a story. In a very small town in the Northwest, the problems of alcohol and teen pregnancy surfaced. The city council members were concerned about their kids and held several meetings to discuss what to do. They started with the logical steps: They consulted experts in teen pregnancy, purchased a very fancy teen-pregnancy prevention program along with drug prevention programs, and paid interesting speakers to give assembly talks to the kids about drugs, alcohol, and teen pregnancy. They spent a lot of money on their prevention efforts.

Evaluation of their efforts after several years showed that the rates of teen pregnancy seemed to be stable—the number of girls who had quit school due to pregnancy hadn't changed. And it appeared that no fewer kids had been using alcohol or drugs. The kids had enjoyed the programs, but the programs had not been effective.

So, the council members held another meeting. They just sort of stared at each other for a few minutes. Then an older rancher, who was sitting with his cowboy-boots feet propped up on a chair, said, "I don't know what to do. It seems like when I was a kid, everyone in town knew us, called us by name, and sort of hooked into our lives. People were real back then, and these problems weren't very common. Maybe we should get to know these kids."

The council members reminisced about their earlier days, and then someone came up with an idea. "Let's hold a town meeting. That wouldn't be hard—there are only about twelve hundred people living here. Let's ask every adult in town to learn the names of every kid. Let's greet them every time we see them and get to know them. Maybe that will have some effect."

The council members weren't overwhelmed with the idea but decided to give it a try. They held a town meeting and presented the idea. The townspeople seemed willing to make the effort. What did they have to lose? It wouldn't cost anything. So, they began to learn names and to nurture relationships with the kids.

Several months after the town started their effort another town meeting was held. There was an enthusiastic buzz in the room where people assembled. They couldn't wait to tell their stories, and every person seemed to have one. People told of the relationships they had developed with youngsters in town—relationships they had begun by just learning the kids' names.

At a school board meeting a couple of years later the registrar mentioned something interesting: "It looks like the number of school dropouts has decreased for some reason. I did some digging, and it actually looks like the number of girls who quit school due to pregnancy has decreased." There were still a few pregnancies among the students, but the improvement was obvious. In fact, in that town, alcohol- and drug-related arrests among the high school kids had also decreased. All of this started when the adults learned the kids' names.

How do you measure whether or not you know the kids well enough? Watch what happens when you see them at the grocery store or some other location. If they see you and simply wave, your relationship with them isn't strong enough. If they see you and actually run to you, you've got it right.

We must transform our church from a church with "the right message" to a church that genuinely cares. This all could start with members learning the names of not only the young people but of everyone who comes through the door of the church.

Can you imagine what would happen if we combined the correct message with the correct love? Are you anxious to hear people say, "Those Adventists are the kindest, most loving people you will ever know?" That's what we all say about Jesus when we get to know Him.

As for me, I'm more overwhelmed and touched by Jesus' love than by the message alone. How about you?

The Church's Role

CHAPTER 2

Coming Home

by Barry Gane

Barry Gane has spent more than thirty years as a youth pastor, teacher, and youth director at union conference and division levels. He directs the Master of Arts in Youth Ministry program at the Seventh-day Adventist Theological Seminary, Berrien Springs, Michigan.

I owe the fact that I'm still in the church to the unconditional love of godly parents and a church family that saw potential that only God could have revealed.

Just after my seventeenth birthday I finally had made the decision to be baptized. At my baptism I hoped the anger, questioning, and disquiet would cease. That things would change—that I would change. I was disappointed to find that nothing had changed, especially not me. Within weeks of my baptism I became further enmeshed with a group of friends and associates that I thought I'd left behind. The bike gang seemed to hold greater appeal than ever. With my last few years in high school still ahead of me, I consciously decided to spend less and less time there and more and more time with the bikers. I left home regularly, telling my parents that I would never return. Instead of acting with anger, they simply let me know that the door was always open.

I was totally self-centered, angry with everyone without a reason—one of those obnoxious kids. There was only one person in my life who mattered to me apart from myself and that was my girlfriend. But eventually I broke up with her and decided to start a completely new life in another state. I took off with just a few dollars in my pocket, a change of clothes, and a sleeping bag and headed west to a new life with an attitude that said, "Anywhere is better than here!" I had a couple of friends who felt the same way; they joined me for the adventure.

Tired of sleeping on the ground and hungry as horses, we arrived in Adelaide, twelve hundred miles from home. One of the guys tried to contact some friends, only to find that they weren't home. We decided to visit anyway; it was an easy house to break into. We thought we'd stay until they came home or one of the neighbors called the police. But the owner of the house was a pastor, and the neighbors must have been used to seeing kids around. Apparently, they thought nothing of us being there.

We ate the food in the fridge but couldn't bring ourselves to sleep in the family's beds. After a few days of sleeping on the floor, I was ready to try something different. I found an old mattress lying out in the backyard and dragged it inside. It smelt a bit, but at least it would be softer than the floor. When we returned to the house in the early hours of the next morning, I just rolled out my sleeping bag on the mattress and fell into an exhausted sleep. But when I awoke the next morning, I discovered my folly—I was covered in fleas. Obviously some animal had used the mattress before me. I had bites all over me; I was scratching the skin off my body. There were so many fleas that the floor seemed to move.

Home started to look pretty good, and I decided that it was time to head back. It took me forty-eight hours of hitchhiking to get there. I was struggling with a savage case of the flu by the time I got home. I was exhausted and hadn't eaten well for a couple weeks. Even though I hadn't slept for a few days, however, the first thing that I did was to ring my girlfriend and ask her whether she'd go out for the night.

"I thought you were never coming back," she said.

"Well, I'm here. Do you want to go out or not?"

"OK."

I asked dad for a loan of the pickup and some cash and headed off to get my girl. We went to a deserted beach and spent hours talking and catching up. Finally, in the early hours of the morning, we headed for home. Not long after we had left the beach, I discovered that we were nearly out of gas. I stopped the car, filled the tank, and then began a desperate search for my wallet. At first I thought it must have fallen down behind the seat or maybe I'd kicked it out on the road somewhere. After an anxious search I went into the gas station and informed the cashier that I'd lost my wallet.

"I hear that story every night; pull the other leg—it whistles. You stay right there. I'm calling the police," he said.

I decided I'd punch his lights out and run for it and hope that he wasn't able to write down the number on my license plate. Then sanity prevailed; I asked, "Why don't you phone my dad?"

He did, and was convinced that my father would pay for the gas. His parting shot at me was, "He seems like a decent man. I don't know where he got you!"

Before the service station attendant could hang up, I grabbed the phone and spoke to my father with uncharacteristic consideration: "Dad, go to bed. Don't wait up for me; I'm coming home. I just want to go down to the beach to try and find my wallet."

As I started the car, I rushed off a simple, unholy prayer, "God, I want the wallet, all right?" There was no "Dear Father" or "Amen," just a rattled demand—more a curse than a prayer. We got back to the beach and began to retrace our steps, eventually arriving at the place where we'd spent most of our time. Running my hand across the sand, I quickly found the wallet. A stroke of good luck!

On the way home I found myself giving in to sleep. Watching the speedometer, mesmerized by it, I caught myself drifting into the curb several times. I begged my girlfriend to talk to me, but by this stage she was exhausted as well, and she lay down across the front seat, her head on my lap, and drifted into deep sleep. I turned the radio up, wound down the window, sang at the top of my lungs, and continued driving—until there was an almighty BANG. When I regained consciousness, I saw sparks dancing across the hood of the car. I looked down and saw that my girlfriend was covered in blood. The engine had come right through the firewall into the seat and appeared to have married itself to her body. I couldn't get out my door, and I couldn't open hers. So eventually I lay on top of her and kicked and kicked until her window exploded. Wriggling through her window, I fell onto the road. Then I struggled to my feet, grabbed her by the legs, pulled her onto the pavement, and dragged her as far away from the crash site as possible.

A Desperate Prayer

People began to flood out of their houses. There weren't any lights, only flashlights—I'd struck a power pole and had knocked out the electricity to the whole area. One of the ladies who came out was a woman whom I knew, a nurse from the local hospital. As I lay there on the ground, blood pumping from my head, my arms, my knee, I looked down and began to realize that my girlfriend had not moved or breathed since I'd pulled her free of the wreck. In desperation I began to ask, "Is Shirley all right? Is she all right?" I was assured that she was fine. Then the people removed me from the scene, propped me up against a tree, and told me to stick a thumb in the side of my head and to put pressure on my knee to stop the bleeding; I'd severed arteries in both places. As I watched, someone brought out a blanket, unfolded it, and completely covered the lifeless form on the ground.

I began to pray for a second time that night, a prayer of absolute desperation. This time it began in the traditional way: "Dear God . . ." The desperate realization flooded over me that I had killed the only person I cared about other than myself. In despair I began to plead with God, but nothing happened. The ambulance arrived and the attendants loaded Shirley into it and made me sit beside her. In the darkness my prayer was even more intense: "Dear God, if You'll do this, then You can have me." What a great deal I was offering God; looking back I can hardly believe that He would even be interested. At the end of my prayer, however, I heard a shrill, blood-curdling scream, the type that only girls can make. It made my hair stand on end, but it was beautiful. Although Shirley didn't regain consciousness at that moment, I knew that she was alive. I rushed off another prayer: "Thanks, Lord."

When we got to the hospital, the nurses began to strip away my clothing and shave the hair from the side of my head. I had nearly lost an ear, and my leg was badly damaged. Just before they began the repair work, my father walked in. I wondered who told him where to find me. He asked whether Shirley and I were going to be all right. The surgeons assured him that there seemed to be no life-threatening damage, although the girl was still not conscious. And then much to my embarrassment he asked if he could pray. I was embarrassed, yet as he prayed I felt something changing in me.

Later, I found out what my father had done that night. Usually when I was out at night he wouldn't go to sleep until I arrived home. That meant many sleepless hours. But this night my dad *had* gone to sleep. He woke up with a start just after 2 A.M., got down on his knees, and for the second time that night prayed for his son who was out there somewhere. He tried to turn on the light and found that there was no electricity, then walked to the kitchen and saw that the electric clock had stopped at the same time that he had awakened. He shook my mother awake, and they headed off to find their son. When he passed his pickup wrapped around the pole just ten miles from home, he drove straight to the hospital, arriving shortly after we did.

Within a few weeks of the accident my girlfriend had mostly recovered, with just minor scarring. I was released from the hospital a little while later. The experience of this wreck was life-changing for me, but I was not back at church. I had not yet submitted to Jesus as Savior, and I didn't recognize Him as Lord. I still had a long way to go.

One Sabbath after I had returned home the family had gone to church, leaving me an invitation to join them. As I crawled under the old wreck of a car I was repairing, it dawned on me that I hadn't fulfilled my promise: "God if You'll do this, You can have me." I thought the first step would be to go back to church. I was still angry and I didn't want to go, so I hatched a plan that would ensure the church's rejection of me. Unwashed, clad in my leathers, black grease through my hair and on my hands, I mounted my motorcycle and roared off to church. I did a couple of wheelies in the parking lot and a few donuts in the dirt. I wanted them to know that I'd arrived. Then I sauntered into the church, sat down in an empty back seat, and looked to the front, expecting to see horror and disgust on the faces of the congregation. Instead I saw tears rolling down my father's cheeks as he sat at the front next to the preacher.

I expected the head deacon, who had two perfect children—one at college, training for the ministry; the other about to marry a church worker—to come over and in a loud voice abuse me and tell me to leave the church: "You should know better; your father is the elder. What are you doing in church dressed like that?"

I had a mouth full of venom, a heart full of bile. I was going to spew all over him and then walk out of the church and say, "God, see I tried, but they didn't want me." But the deacon didn't come.

The sermon dragged on. Finally the agony ended and people began to walk down the aisle. They put their hands on my shoulders and told me how good it was to see me in church. This wasn't what I expected; it wasn't what I wanted.

As I walked to the door, I shook hands with my dad. I could see him swallowing hard. He said nothing, but the handshake spoke volumes. I placed my greasy hand in the hand of the pastor, and I could see the start of the reaction I wanted. But he bit his tongue and said nothing.

Then, as I walked down the steps at the front of the church, I saw the deacon coming. *He's kept it 'til now,* I thought. I was sure that he was going to hit me, so I decided to "king hit" him and then run and hope like mad that the motorcycle would start before the rest of the deacons got to me. But instead of a closed fist, he reached out an open hand. And as he pumped my arm, he told me how thrilled he was that I was back at church. No sooner had he let go of my hand than a little man who stood only as high as my chin threw his arms around me and began to weep on my shoulder and say, "Welcome home." He assured me of his prayers and how he had longed for the day that I would come back.

As I stood there, a nineteen-year-old, I felt awkward and embarrassed, but strangely warm. That was my first day back at church, and I have never missed since. It took a while for God to change my exterior, but His Spirit had really begun to work internally.

It was the unconditional love of my parents and the support of a church that really was family, that understood community and acceptance, that finally broke through my shell of anger and alienation and helped me realize how important I was in the eyes of God.

CHAPTER 3

How a Large Church Involves the Youth

by Karl Haffner

Karl Haffner is senior pastor of the Walla Walla College Church. He is also the founder and lead pastor of an alternative church option called the Improv Church. Myrna Tetz interviewed him.

MT: When I visited your church, three twelve-year-old girls led the singing at the beginning of the church service, a teenager played a solo for the offertory, and another teenager played the organ. I know you have exceptional professionals available for every aspect of your church service. Why do you use young people?

KH: We use young people because our mission is not to present flawless performances or to always hit the right notes on the organ or to curtail all whispering at the pulpit. Over and over in board meetings and staff meetings I've heard it said, "Because this is a college church, students are at the heart of our mission. That's where our energies and resources need to flow." I wholeheartedly agree with and preach that sentiment.

Our mission comes from Matthew 28, which says that Jesus called us to go into all the world and preach the gospel, baptizing those who respond in the name of the Father, Son, and Holy Ghost. We believe this starts with those within arm's reach—our kids. We recognize that one of the most effective ways to assimilate kids into the church is to beg for their involvement. People learn at a much deeper level when they participate rather than watch.

My personal experience validates this. As I reflect on roughly eighteen years of attending a local church where my dad served as pastor, two services float to the top in my memories. The first was the week the local head elder requested that I offer the main prayer. That Sabbath prayer occurred thirty-one years ago, and yet it's tattooed on my brain still. Why? Because I was involved.

The other Sabbath that is most memorable in my childhood happened when I was in seventh grade. The head deacon approached me and said, "Karl, I think you have a gift for public speaking. Would you be willing to preach some Sabbath?"

I was stunned by the request. "What about the pastor? Don't you reckon he'd be bent out of shape if I took his pulpit some week?"

"Nonsense. I'll talk to the pastor—I think your dad will work with me on this one."

Recently I dusted off that sermon and read it. I blushed with embarrassment to think I would preach anything so shallow and boring. I'm sure it was a lot harder to listen to than a few missed notes on the organ. But at that time the church members at the Roanoke Seventh-day Adventist Church fully embraced me and encouraged me to pursue a career in preaching. Of course, that's exactly what I did.

Those two Sabbaths were the most spiritually defining experiences of my childhood. That's why I'm committed to creating the same kinds of experiences for the young people in my church.

Too many people feel like their impact in worship is the equivalent of an extra gallon of water spilling over Niagara Falls—as if their small contribution doesn't matter. Paul tells us that everyone is a contributor: seventh-graders, first-graders, professionals, and senior citizens. Everyone has a hymn or a word of instruction; a revelation, a tongue, or an interpretation. True biblical worship demands that each of us have something to contribute in worship. If we are serious about retaining the next generation for Christ, then we need more deacons challenging seventh-graders to use their gifts for God, because every person must be a contributor.

MT: You gave some startling statistics in a sermon recently. How do these numbers affect you, your church members, and your ministry?

KH: The Adventist Church is facing a monumental crisis. Consider with me the trends of worship attendance over the past thirty years. In 1965, the membership in the North American Division was 370,000. Of that membership, 300,000 were regular attendees. (Regular attendees were defined at the time as members who would come to church at least three times a month.) The average age was 35.

Only twenty years later, in 1985, the membership in North America had doubled—700,000. Praise the Lord! But there was a decline in worship attendance, to only 325,000. Now that may not seem so catastrophic until you factor into the equation that the definition of "regular attendance" was modified. It was now defined as people who would come to church just once a month.

By 1995 our membership eclipsed 815,000—but the average total attendance each Sabbath plummeted to a dismal 265,000. We have almost tripled our membership since 1965, but our attendance is significantly less. And while the average age of our attendees back in 1965 was 35, in 1995 it had jumped to 65. What does that tell you about what is happening in our church?

Ministry magazine published a similar study and concluded with this statement: "The 'Youth Retention Study' by Roger Dudley reveals that Adventist young adults . . . generally have negative attitudes toward their local congregations. . . . An estimated 36 percent have already essentially left the church, and others are soon to follow."

Over a third of our Adventist young adults have already left the church, with others soon to follow! I don't know about you, but that's the kind of thing that keeps me awake at night. I toss and turn in my bed, wondering, *How are we going to stop the bleeding and recapture the interest of our young adults in this Adventist movement?*

I hope you can sense the spirit in which I share this. I have a passion for the next generation. This is their church. I say, "Come, however you feel comfortable. However you dress, however you sing, however you smell. You are not only welcome, but you are the very heart of this congregation, and we need you. It's not just that we want you here. It's not just that we like you here. We need you."

MT: Your church is the home for the 1,500 college students and 300 academy students. What is your concept of ministry to these age groups?

KH: In a word, "involvement." Rather than thinking of our role as ministering to these young people, we think long and hard about ways we can invite them to minister in community with us. We want them to think they're in this adventure of fulfilling the Great Commission (Matthew 28) with us. So, we have brainstormed ways to connect the generations and minister together. Here's a list of twenty ideas that we've compiled in an attempt to include all age groups but particularly collegians, since we're a college church:

- Put students on all committees.
- Involve students in leadership roles in all Sabbath Schools and clubs such as Pathfinders.
- Involve students on the team that plans worship services and in the worship services themselves.
- Conduct regular Festivals of Ministries throughout the year. (This involves setting up ministry booths where students can sign up to be involved in whatever ministry interests them.)
- Form small groups that are intergenerational that study through the same passages that the pastor will cover on Sabbath mornings in a pulpit series. (This way we have older and younger generations connecting over food and conversation about the same topic as the sermon the upcoming Sabbath.)
- Sponsor "We-haul." (Church members greet incoming students with freshly baked cookies or other treats and help them to move their boxes into their dorm rooms.)
- Include testimonies from people of all generations in the worship service.
- Sponsor intergenerational retreats and socials.
- Coordinate "Bring a student home for lunch." (This systematically targets students in the congregation to make sure they get an invitation to join church members for Sabbath lunch.)
- Encourage students to participate in the church's Adopt-a-grandparent program.

- Sponsor short-term mission trips that are intergenerational.
- Continue to sponsor the Improv Church—a student-driven evangelistic outreach to other colleges in the community.
- Encourage members to "Adopt-a-hall" (Adult members "adopt" a dormitory hall, bringing treats, hanging out with the students, etc., weekly.)
- Encourage members to attend college functions like chapel services, Week of Prayer meetings, etc.
- Offer intergenerational prayer groups every day at the church.
- Establish a mentoring program for student elders.
- Have our parish nurses visit students who are ill.
- Preach regularly on the topic of the importance of all ages being involved in our church.
- Include times during the worship service during which members can mingle and meet new people.
- Offer Saturday night "game nights" for all ages to get together over table games.

MT: Do you have any training models for the older young people to minister to the younger ones?

KH: Yes, we have some of the best! Our youth pastor, Troy Fitzgerald, has published an outstanding series of guides called "Christwise." These guides are especially designed to help older students to journey spiritually with younger students. (These guides are available through Adventist Book Centers.)

MT: How important do you believe your children's divisions to be?

KH: Moderately important. This is not to suggest that our children are not important—they are the highest priority in our church. However, I don't believe that segregating generations is the healthiest model for church involvement. While I do believe it's a very good thing to present the gospel to kids in a manner that is age-appropriate, I think it's just as important to get the kids and the parents and the grandparents centered on spiritual activities to foster a sense of intergenerational community.

MT: Other than leading or assisting in the children's divisions, what role could adults play in ministry to the children that would have a positive effect on the children's view of the church?

KH: I'm big on tackling all-church projects that can't be pulled off without everyone (all ages included) pitching in. For example, in my first church we had an annual living-nativity drive-thru. When it became a traffic-stopping event that attracted up to eight thousand community members, it required all 150 of our members to pull it off. While this was a great benefit to the community, I believe it was just as helpful to our own church members, because it put ten-year-olds in the parking lot with grandpas to help direct traffic. It put the young adults who played Joseph and Mary at the manger scene. Not only was there a place for everyone to work together in the church, we needed everyone to pull it off. I think the best ministry to our children is to work with them in doing outreach to the community.

MT: What criteria do you have for those who present the children's story?

KH: We have ten guidelines—things like keep it under five minutes and coordinate thematically with the sermon. We choose storytellers primarily based on past experiences, people who have demonstrated competency in this area. We do ask some adults to join the kids to help control the hundred or so kids who come up. We also feel that makes a nice inter-generational statement.

MT: What do you believe is the single most important ministry to the children and young people in your congregation?

KH: The ministry of invitation: "Hey, Junior, would you help me present Communion to some of our older members this Sabbath afternoon? I'll pick you up at two o'clock." Or: "Hey, Susie, would you do the church a big favor by volunteering down at our Community Service Center this Sunday?" That kind of thing.

MT: Do you believe the sermon time is specifically a time for the older people and the very young should learn to sit quietly?

KH: I absolutely believe the sermon should connect with all generations. The primary way I attempt to do this is through stories that all generations can relate to. Such stories exist, and I believe they can be used to connect the generations.

That we try everything we can to pass on the Adventist message of grace to the next generation is not negotiable. We have to do it. We have to do it because there are thousands of precious young people just like twenty-four-year-old Hannah, who wrote this letter:

> My generation and I are often misjudged. . . . Because of my youth, I was labeled as being part of the "new generation," the rebels. I have never felt like a rebel—not until now. . . .
>
> The funny thing is, the standards I have chosen are closer to "old day church standards" than my elder church members suspect. So, it appears that they think I am worse off than I really am. Unlike [what] my fellow church members think, my generation doesn't hate Ellen White. We take care of our bodies. We want to help the community and world around us be a better place. We are not trying to [be] corrupt. We are taking our relationships with Christ seriously. We want to know God.
>
> Unfortunately, we get bogged down in the muck of church politics and board meetings with our elders. The truth: We would like to be free of all the busyness and actually get busy. We are tired of sitting and not doing. We ARE willing to work, but often our hands are tied because church traditions of "sitting and talking and voting before doing" are still around. We want to work. We are ready. Please ask us to get busy, but don't ask us to be busy being busy. I believe Christ was a rebel. He didn't jump through the hoops or go through the red tape. He just got busy touching people's lives. I want to be a rebel.

I want to be a rebel with Hannah. And I want to be a part of the leadership that unleashes her generation for the cause of Christ.

CHAPTER 4

The Whole Body of Christ

by Ryan J. Bell

Ryan J. Bell is pastor of the Bucks County Seventh-day Adventist Church in Pennsylvania. He and his church members are committed to making their church a safe place for young and old alike to grow and explore their faith together.

Two formative experiences shaped my view regarding children and youth and the church's role in nurturing their spiritual life. The initial formative experience occurred during the first month after I began working as a pastor. To me, the incident was so insignificant that I didn't even notice it when it happened. The wife of one of the church's elders told me about it later that day.

The elder had invited me home for lunch that Sabbath. During that afternoon, his wife said that I had made a great impression on her son. I quickly scanned my short-term memory for some idea of how I could have been so impressive. Coming up with nothing, I asked, "What did I do?"

With a grin on her face she said, "Well, Jeff said to me on the way home, 'The new pastor is cool!' When I asked him what he meant he said that you had talked to him."

I talked to him? Well, yes, I *had* talked to him—that I remembered. But what's the big deal? The conversation was pretty typical for two young men:

"Hey, Jeff, how ya doin'?"

"Good."

"That's good! Happy Sabbath."

"You too."

At that point I was less confused and more confused. I was less confused about why I didn't remember having impressed Jeff. I was more confused about why he thought I was so "cool" just because I had talked to him. Didn't all pastors talk to people? Isn't that a pastor's job? What had I done that was so remarkable?

As I have gotten a little older and more experienced, I have learned that there are pastors who avoid talking to the young people in their churches. In fact, many adults in general *fear* interacting with the kids in the church, especially those between the ages of thirteen and twenty-one. When you are young, you look like the other young people. But as you get older, the clothing and hairstyle, music and slang, activities and values of the young all look as strange as if the young people had just emigrated from Mongolia. As a rule, we tend to fear what we don't understand—so, most adults fear the kids in their church.

If you don't think this is true, measure your reaction the next time you run across a young man with hair an unnatural color, pants so baggy you could put two of him in them, headphones surgically attached to his head, black fingernail polish, and so many piercings he looks like a piece of Swiss cheese. Are you not a little reticent to engage him in a conversation? Are you not a little afraid of him? You may even judge him to be "bad" just by the way he looks. Add to that the fact that more and more children—yes, *children*—are committing serious crimes that have historically been the province of adults. So, let's not fool ourselves, adults today fear kids.

But this fear is not unavoidable. What is needed is understanding and love. Young people need attention, affirming, mentoring, and love just like older folk do. With that kind of exchange there is no room for fear, because "perfect love banishes fear" (1 John 4:18, NEB).

Young People as People

The day Jeff thought I was "cool" I learned something: *Young people are people.* That may seem like a simple statement of fact. However, judging by the way some churches relate to young people, one could easily conclude that church is for adults—the only people that matter.

This is not surprising, given the degree to which our society pigeonholes people and separates them into countless demographic segments. There are, we are told, Builders, Silents, Baby Boomers, Baby Busters (or GenXers), and Millennials (or 13th Gen). And there are countless products and services specifically marketed to each of these segments.

If there is one thing that is true about our postmodern society, it is that we are fragmented. Our society divides us. Families rarely eat together, play together, or work together. The proverbial "soccer mom" demonstrates this. She wakes early to see that the kids have their clothes on straight and their faces washed for school. The family may meet momentarily over a bowl of cereal to get their respective schedules for the day synchronized; then they're out the door. Mom drops one kid off at school on the way to her part-time job; Dad takes the other one. In the afternoon Mom picks up both kids, drops one off at soccer practice and just barely gets the other one to music lessons. She has just enough time to run errands—grocery store, post office, bank—before she has to pick them up. The kids do homework until bedtime. Dad supervises the kids while Mom heads off to the church for a meeting. Finally, husband and wife collapse into bed at 11 P.M. For many, this is just life. They rarely spend any time together as a family.

When this family goes to church, what do they find? Ministries for women, ministries for men, ministries for children, youth, collegiate young people, young adults, young professionals, single adults, divorced adults, empty nesters, and senior citizens. Some churches have taken this market segmentation so far that they have entire churches made up of one demographic group. In the same way, some churches have formed around a particular age group; you can find youth churches, young adult churches, and baby boomer churches.

Common experience and language make these various ministries and churches desirable in many ways. However, I can't help but think that this is not the body of Christ in its fullest sense. When people are divided from each other by external boundaries, something vital is lost. Churches need grandparents, parents, and youth. Churches need Asians, Africans, Hispanics, Europeans, and Americans of every stripe to help maintain a balanced view of God and His mission in the world. A crucial part of Christian discipleship is learning to get along with people who are different. When the church is too one-sided, this discipleship is short-circuited. I have found this to be so true that I now intentionally lead my church to be increasingly intergenerational and multicultural.

A Fresh Look at Children's and Youth Ministry

So, how do we seek the kind of Christian communion that Jesus had in mind?

Think of your children and unbaptized youth as members. Of course, they are not *technically* members of the church, but they *are* members of the body.

Baby dedications can teach this important value to the congregation. There is really a three-fold dedication being made:

1. The parents are dedicating the child to the Lord.
2. The parents are dedicating themselves to the Lord.
3. The congregation is dedicating themselves to the Lord by promising to assist in the raising of their children by making sure the church is a healthy place for kids.

The pastor can make every baby dedication a reminder to the congregation that children are *members*. They may not be on the official rolls of the church, but they are vital to the health and growth of the church. A church with no children is doomed to die.

Rather than assigning your young people "their own place," help them connect to the whole life of the congregation. Churches easily get in the habit of viewing their young people as a problem. They may lament, "What are we going to do about our young people?" or pray that the Lord will "help our young people." It's not that we shouldn't pray for our kids—we must! But I often wonder if congregations think God is going to save their young people over the church's strident efforts to keep them out of the center of church life.

The most common solution to the "What are we going to do with our young people?" question is to create a youth group and, if possible, hire a youth pastor. While these may be helpful, the church board may just be "throwing them a bone"—giving them something they'll like so they'll leave the adults alone. The adults, then, can get back to their church as they know it, and the kids can have a good time while they are learning something about Jesus.

Mark DeVries says, "Over the last century churches and parachurch youth ministries alike have increasingly (and often unwittingly) held to a single strategy that has become the most common characteristic of the model: the isolation of teenagers from the adult world and particularly from their own parents" (*Family-Based Youth Ministry,* p. 21). This makes the body of Christ something less than it was meant to be, and it short-circuits the discipleship process for our kids.

So, give your young people opportunities for real leadership and not just token involvement. Nominating committees are notorious for wanting to "get the young people involved" by putting one or two on every committee. In this way members appease their consciences by saying that their kids are involved without really releasing to them the possibility of changing something.

What if we monitored our young people's growth, helped them understand their spiritual gifts and special abilities, and then gradually mentored them into the *leadership* of some ministry? Or better, what if we helped them develop a new ministry that is close to their heart?

Focus on helping your young people develop an adult faith. A steady diet of youth ministry programming may help our kids come to know Jesus and experience Him as a real presence in their lives, but it may also prevent them from making the transition to a mature faith. Intentional steps must be taken to integrate them into the life of the church. We cannot be caught saying, even to ourselves, "They have their youth group. What else do they want?"

DeVries cites numerous examples in his book to support his thesis—"Successful youth ministries do not necessarily produce mature

Christian adults." What exactly is the difference between a childlike faith and a mature faith? A childlike faith sees everything in black-and-white. ("Bad things don't happen to good people." "Jesus always answers my prayers." "Good Christians are always strong.") Mature faith realizes that life is not quite so neat and tidy, that the mental categories we put everything into when we were kids don't really hold all the problems of life—that there is a good deal of gray between the black-and-white.

The reality is that one day our young people will grow up and leave home for college. When they do, will they have the spiritual resources to stay connected to God and the church? Will we have been successful at helping our kids move from the faith of their parents to their own personal faith? This is our task. No one else will do it for us.

The Second Experience

My second formative "youth ministry" experience came only a few years after the first. We had recently changed the worship format and were involving more people in leading the worship service. We had someone on the piano, a couple of people on guitars, someone operated an overhead projector, and three or four people led the congregation in singing. Hearing of this change, our conference president came to see for himself.

A couple of weeks later I read in the conference newsletter a report from the president that said that our church was doing "something innovative in youth ministry." This piqued my interest; I didn't know of anything innovative we were doing in youth ministry. In fact, we didn't even have a "youth ministry" per se.

The president's report said that our young people were involved in all the different aspects of the worship service—singing, playing instruments, running the overheads, running the sound system. He had interpreted this as youth ministry. I suppose we did give intentional thought to involving our young people in worship, but we thought of them as church members with gifts and talents—not as token young people up front to appease consciences.

God had blessed our church with the ability to see our young people as people and full members of the church, and for this we were grateful. There wasn't a need to create a separate worship service for the young people. Instead, a worship service was designed with all our members in mind that utilized all our members' gifts. Our young people felt that the church was their church too, and visitors, like our conference president, noticed the difference.

It's a good idea to take the time to talk to the young people in your church. It doesn't take much—just talk to them and get to know what their interests are. Then design your children's and youth ministry in such a way that it facilitates their involvement in the full life of the church. Don't allow church to be one more way our society fragments our families.

Gary Hopkins's comments:

Does your church's nominating committee have to beg to get leaders for the children and youth divisions every year? Try this—quit having adult Sabbath School and send everyone to these divisions to interact with the kids!

The truth is that today, in this fragmented society, our children and young people need to develop resilience—the capacity to maintain competent functioning in the face of major life stressors. Upon a careful review of much of the available research designed to identify what fosters resiliency, we see one factor that emerges over and over again: valuable, sincere, and enduring relationships. Let's each focus on being that person, that adult, who loves and cares for the children and youth in our church and in our communities.

See: R. Brooks, "Children at Risk: Fostering Resilience and Hope," *American Journal of Orthopsychiatry,* 1994, 64 (4), 545–553; and T. P. Herbert, "Portraits of Resilience: The Urban Life Experience of Gifted Latino Young Men" *Roeper Review,* December 1996, 19 (2), 82–91.

CHAPTER 5

Home, Sweet Home

by Stephen Chavez

Stephen Chavez is managing editor of the Adventist Review, Silver Spring, Maryland. On Sabbath mornings he is a "benevolent dictator" to between twenty and thirty seventh- and eighth-graders at the Sligo Seventh-day Adventist Church in Takoma Park, Maryland.

The words "I grew up in the church" are often heard wherever Adventists gather. We know what the speaker means. He or she doesn't mean that they literally grew up sleeping in the Sabbath School rooms, taking their meals in the fellowship hall, or using the baptistry for their weekly baths. They mean that their earliest memories are so intertwined with church that its members were a kind of surrogate family and the significant events of their lives—dedications, baptisms, graduations, weddings, funerals, etc.—provided kind of a home away from home. In my case, one of the most vivid memories of my childhood involves the time-honored tradition of doodling on the church bulletin.

The back page of the bulletins used in the church in which I grew up (see, I did it myself) were often blank—perfect for artistic renderings of animals, boats, cars, planes, or whatever other subjects were on the mind of an elementary-school-age boy. One Sabbath I used that space to draw a picture of the outside of the church. For some reason I decided to hand my masterpiece to the pastor as he stood shaking parishioners' hands as they exited the sanctuary.

The next week I received an envelope in the mail addressed to "Master Steve Chavez," and in it, on radiant, white church stationery, the pastor thanked me for sharing with him my "gift." He said he hoped I'd continue to develop my artistic talents; that God would surely bless me as I dedicated my life to Him.

To say it was memorable is a vast understatement. Until that day I thought I was invisible to all but my parents and the Sabbath School teachers. To think that someone as important as the pastor would notice me—even send me a letter on church stationery—well, it made an impression I'll never forget.

A Pastor's Plan

Given the choice of teaching a Sabbath School class of adults or children, I'll choose children every time—they're so full of energy and creativity. And when I look at a child's face, I can't help imagining them as adults, wondering what choices they'll make as they grow older, form friendships, and choose careers, spouses, and avenues of service to God. Childhood is a formative time for virtually all of a person's decisions. So as a pastor, I want to be as influential as any other voice children will listen to. Over the years I've used several techniques to reach the kids in my church and let them know that I'm looking out for them.

Names. Obviously! As adults, we know how important it is to be remembered by name; how off-putting it is to have to remind somebody of our name every time we see them. I try to remember kids' names. I use them when I see them, not only at church, but at other activities as well. And speaking of other activities, I've learned that kids really appreciate an adult's presence in their lives outside of church. As often as my schedule allows, I go to recitals, basketball games, track meets, church socials—wherever I'm likely to meet kids.

Knowing kids' names represents knowing enough about those kids to know their parents and something of their home life, their hobbies and interests. The pastor who sent me that letter about my bulletin artwork also showed up at my front door one day after school. I had mentioned that my friends and I had noticed a beehive in the trees near our house, and the pastor, a bee keeper, asked me to help him capture them. The attempt was ultimately unsuccessful, but it gave me a bonding experience with the man who would later lead me into the baptistry as I made a public demonstration of my commitment to Jesus.

Presence. I spent nine years of my pastoral ministry in a parish with a one-room school. The school had a yearly tradition called "Outdoor Education." It meant that for a week or ten days every spring, the students, teachers, a few parents, and the pastor would travel to some "exotic" location—the mountains, seashore, desert, or some combination of the three—to learn lessons from God's great outdoors.

Because I play the guitar and can tell a pretty good story, I was always involved in outdoor education. The days spent mountain climbing, canoeing, and swimming; the nights spent sleeping in rustic cabins and on gymnasium floors; and the meals of grilled-cheese sandwiches and chips, macaroni-and-cheese and chips, beans and cheese and chips, chips and chips, etc., in all kinds of weather, are an indelible part of the memories of scores of kids. On those trips the kids learned that Christianity is not only practiced in church on Sabbath or at Wednesday evening prayer meeting. Christianity translates to the world of travel, weather delays, car trouble, car sickness, and emergency bathroom breaks on the side of the road.

Short-term mission trips also provide valuable opportunities for adults to model Christian characters far beyond the confines of the church. Young people have made many a life-changing decision when faced with a combination of the world's need, Christian concern, and the power of Christian fellowship and cooperation.

Humor. "Hi, my name is Steve," I tell kids when I meet them for the first time. "But you can call me Steve."

Kids have a finely tuned sense of humor, and they appreciate humor in adults. In our Earliteen Sabbath School we try to cultivate a climate in which kids realize they're not entering the "no-humor zone." Adults sometimes think they're preserving reverence if they make Sabbath services boring and joyless. But Jesus appreciated humor (read carefully some of His sermons and stories), and those of us who are leading kids will also cultivate a sense of humor that capitalizes on the joy of life and the humor of a well-turned phrase.

I prefer my humor dry. When I welcome a visitor to our Maryland Sabbath School class, and she says she's visiting from California, I might say, "You must've gotten up really early this morning."

"We flew in Wednesday."

"Are your arms still tired?" (It's an old joke, but seventh- and eighth-graders love it.)

Often when a kid enters the room I offer my hand and the greeting, "Happy Sabbath." When the kid grabs my hand I keep pumping his arm as I comment about what he's wearing and ask him questions about his week. When he tries to pull away, I keep holding on. "Let go of my hand," I'll say. "Let go of *my* hand," he'll say. "You're the one holding on to me," I'll maintain.

We never allow our humor to turn mean or ugly; there's too much of that in the real world. We have fun because we always make a point of laughing *with* someone, not *at* them. Humor is like a flame. When it's under control, it can be effective in communicating and creating a comfortable atmosphere. But it can be disruptive when it gets out of control. And the difference between in control and out of control is sometimes a delicate one.

Tokens. Kids are almost always "invisible" church members. Think about it: The only time we typically notice kids is when they're in trouble or making too much noise. Yet by ministering to children, we're not only ministering to them, we're ministering to their parents and their entire extended family as well.

Whenever a young person leads out in the worship service—singing, praying, reading the Scripture—I send little notes of appreciation, encouraging their future participation in church life. Whenever I hear about someone doing something significant in school or in the community—being elected a class officer, winning an essay contest, performing at a recital—I mail her or him a congratulatory message. All the leaders of my Earliteen Sabbath School class send personally signed birthday cards to all the kids on their birthdays.

Incidentally, it's vital that kids who don't go to Adventist schools or live in Adventist homes get extra support from their church family. In many ways, they're swimming against the current.

When I was a parish pastor, I always carried rolls of Lifesavers in my suit pocket every Sabbath morning. (Thank you, Costco!) Then, while shaking hands at the conclusion of a worship service, I greeted all the kids with a Lifesaver and the words "Thanks for being quiet in church."

Sometimes parents said, "Oh, but he wasn't quiet today."

Then I said to the child, "You'll be quiet next week, won't you?"

Grace. There's not much real grace in today's world. We can preach it all we want, but kids know whether it's just a word or a reality in our life. Early in my pastoral ministry I made mistakes that reflected a rather graceless orientation. Unfortunately, history can't be unwritten. But with the aid of hindsight and a better grasp of the gospel in my own life, I'm determined to create a climate in my church in which kids experience grace first-hand.

Not long ago one of the kids in my Earliteen Sabbath School class became so disruptive that his continued presence was keeping the other kids from learning anything. So I stopped in mid-thought and told him it was time for him to go. There was no scene, no gnashing of teeth, just a quiet calm when the kids realized I meant business.

Later, after the worship service, I met the same young man in the balcony. As I shook his hand, I slipped him some candy (I still keep some in my pocket) and told him that I bore no hard feelings. Then I said, "See you next week." He's gone on to academy, but when we meet, I still know his name, and we still chat about what he's up to.

Once I had to apologize to one of the Earliteens for something that happened in Sabbath School. Cultivating a climate of grace not only means being gracious, it also means (when the situation demands it) being humble enough to ask for forgiveness. I may be mistaken, but that may be the kind of demonstration kids see far too little of these days.

What we're trying to create is a sanctuary (small "s") where kids feel safe when they know they've messed up; where they can have someone take them seriously; where they can ask hard questions while not necessarily looking for answers, maybe just check our reactions to their questions.

In many ways, the kids growing up in our homes and churches are far more sophisticated than we were at the same age. Yet underneath their apparently careless and sometimes callous attitudes are young souls trying (like the rest of us) to figure out the answers to life's great questions: Where did I come from? Why am I here? Where am I going?

Fortunately, we have answers to these and other questions. But in order for them to hear our answers, our experience has to correspond with our profession. Kids are remarkably intuitive. They know if our practice doesn't match our preaching.

CHAPTER 6

Growing Effective Churches That Meet Needs
by Doug Kilcher

Doug Kilcher is the ministerial director of the Mid-America Union Conference of Seventh-day Adventists, Lincoln, Nebraska. He says that every vibrant church that is on fire has turned its young people loose to lead their church to the next level of effectiveness.

Donald Morgan had been pastor of the old, historic church for only a few months. He had been called by the congregation as a last resort before the church closed its doors. The church was a gorgeous colonial meetinghouse located in the center of town, but fewer and fewer people attended.

Pastor Morgan liked to walk down to the village for lunch and then walk back to the church, asking himself as the church came into view, "What does this church say to those who see it? How can it meet the needs of the neighborhood?" One day he was walking on the sidewalk across the street from the church when a young man, apparently a tourist, stopped him, and, gesturing toward the church, asked, "Tell me, sir, is that a church or a museum?" Pastor Morgan said that he was devastated by the implications of the question. He responded to the young man with fervent passion, "I hope to God it is a church!" It was an event that became a defining moment in the church's life; it helped that congregation begin a journey toward effectiveness and growth.[1]

The Importance of Leadership

"Pastors must lead if churches are to change."[2] But therein lies a huge problem. More than 40 percent of those taking a recent survey said they want their pastor/lay leader to be cooperative, caring, and honest, while only 3 percent said they valued more highly the characteristics of competence, independence, determination, courage, maturity, fair-mindedness, dependability, forward-looking attitude, imagination, and ambition.[3] The characteristics appreciated by the 40 percent serve well if clergy are expected simply to maintain the status quo. But if pastors/lay leaders are expected to drive the congregation's mission forward, they must have courage.

Enter the world of management verses leadership. To *manage* means "to bring about, to accomplish, to have charge of or responsibility for, to conduct." *Leading* is "influencing, guiding in direction, course, action, opinion."[4] The distinction is crucial. Warren Bennis and Burt Nanus have written extensively on the "look" of leadership. They say, "The problem with many organizations, and especially the ones that are failing, is that they tend to be overmanaged and underled."[5] They show that there is a large difference between management and leadership. Both are important. But congregations must have leadership or they wallow. *Managers are people who do things right, and leaders are people who do the right thing.* The distinction is a matter of efficiency versus effectiveness.

Making decisions and moving ahead is risky. Feelings may be hurt. Power and influence may shift. Growth may bring new faces with more challenges. But the alternative is worse: Death! The gospel commission compels us to find the people who want to grow spiritually and to prepare them for the second coming of Jesus. Anything less is unacceptable. This is the crux of the issue regarding church health and vitality.

It is generally acknowledged that leadership is more of an art than a science. Groups that want change must confer authority upon the leader. Otherwise, the leader may work extremely hard, but the members will sit on the sidelines, not participating in programs that make a difference in the gospel harvest. Paul wrote about how deeply he cared for his church members (see 1 Thess. 2:8). But caring deeply poses dangers too. It can lead to inactivity because decisions and changes threaten to end relationships when people take a "do or die" stand against transformation.

What then is the leader's responsibility in the turnaround journey in a church? Leaders must understand the stages of change that people go through and patiently guide them through these stages, not allowing derailment by threats, anger, or intimidation. Many churches have been in recline and decline for years. It takes unending encouragement and prodding to see change. Yes, prayer, spirituality, sense of humor, and people skills are very important. But once a leader has clearly articulated a vision—such as the development of ministries to children and youth—and allowed the members to reshape the vision, then it is time to call for a vote and follow through with a decision. That's a difficult thing for the members of a declining church to do. Often, they consider the risk too great, and the church remains stuck until it dies.

The Difference Between Growing and Declining Churches

In 2001, the Mid-America Union Conference completed a study of 109 Adventist churches—fifty-five of the fastest growing churches and fifty-four of the fastest declining churches. The growing churches differed from the declining churches in four ways:

1. Vision
    a. The growing church has a clear concept of the future.
    b. It is willing to create the future instead of allowing the future to determine its viability.
2. Vitality
    a. The pastor has a clear vision for the church and can lead people toward a goal.
    b. The church has the capacity to do ministry in the community.
    c. The church has a population that's relatively large and stable with which to work.
3. Values
    a. The church values the lost.
    b. The cultures of the church, community, and pastor match.
    c. The church places high priority on young people and youth activities.

4. Validation
   a. It is clearly evident that God has been at work in the church during the past two years.
   b. There are no issues of unresolved sin or conflict in the congregation.

The study found fifteen additional markers that distinguish growing churches from declining churches. Growing churches:

1. Have pastor(s) and members who are involved in community activities.
2. Are located in towns with a population of 2,500 or more.
3. Are located less than ten miles from a Wal-Mart store.
4. Are located in area in which the population is in transition: people are moving in and out.
5. Are pastored by relatively young individuals.
6. Are "very friendly" (as contrasted with "friendly").
7. Are open to change and new methods.
8. Make outreach and evangelism the number one priority of both the church and the pastor.
9. Maintain an atmosphere that is open and safe for visitors.
10. Deliver multiple children's programs.
11. Mentor and train new members.
12. Involve a relatively high percentage of members in ministry.
13. Have a pastor whose strongest skill is evangelism (as contrasted with third strongest for pastors of declining churches).
14. Welcome and treat guests as if they are members.
15. Have written plans and goals.

Upon reading this information, pastors/lay leaders could easily conclude that because their church doesn't have some of the markers, "we don't fit the profile of churches that can grow, so there's little hope for us." But there is hope—great hope. It lies in the fact that a church can once again become effective in the harvest if it searches for God's vision for them.

A church of fifteen members can ask the Lord for opportunities to find lost people in their area. They can make plans to try different forms of ministry, such as offering free car washes, free oil changes for single moms, or some other free service. Of course, they would involve their young people in every ministry they planned and carried out.

A church of 175 members can offer to remove snow from driveways and sidewalks near the church, hold a Mother's Day carnation giveaway outside a grocery store, dry cars at self-serve car washes, rake leaves, offer free Christmas gift wrapping, or give away popsicles at store exits during the hot summer months—all free of charge, of course. Showing God's love in practical ways will open avenues to build relationships with others. Our service to others should be free to them. Consider what Jesus did for us! He gave of Himself on Calvary so we need not pay that price. We need to be humble and grateful for that fact. We serve others because of His free gift to us.

As we serve other people, we begin to understand and appreciate them. This is a great way to keep the young people involved and show them how "real" Christians look and live. We may later have the opportunity to share spiritually with the people we served physically. This is how churches grow.

The Journey to Transforming Your Church

The word *transformation* describes a healthy congregation. *Transformation* is based on Latin roots that mean "to change across form." Plants derive oxygen from carbon dioxide in a process of transformation. Healthy congregations serve the gospel by being communities in which faith transforms individual members so that they are motivated to share with those who do not know the Lord Jesus Christ. I believe Paul had this in mind when he wrote Romans 12:2, "Be transformed by the renewing of your mind" (NIV).

How can you transform your church so that it listens and speaks in ways that meet the spiritual needs of today's generation?

Step One: Seek God's vision, not the pastor's, for your church through prayer, fasting, and listening. Vision is what the leaders (lay and pastor) are willing to die for. It is never a program, financial goal, or policy statement. It is a map to the future, the preferred future. It must be realistic, flexible, clear, and very simple. Vision includes mission and values statements. Finding it must involve young people. It generally takes two to four years to seek and receive God's specific vision for your congregation.

Step Two: Create a sense of urgency. We become complacent very quickly. Someone has suggested that the vision of the church must be articulated every twenty-six days or it is lost. Graph the membership of the church over the past twenty years and then continue the line into the future. The message will be clear. If the graph is flat, remind the church that the ultimate outcome is the same as that of a human body that has a flat-line EKG.

Step Three: Engage a core group of the congregational leadership, including young people, who share the leader's passion for spiritual and numerical growth. No football team can win if only the quarterback is committed. Churches that seek transformation must have a team of leaders to refine vision, communicate to everyone, eliminate the obstacles, lead the projects, run interference, and institutionalize the change.

Step Four: Cast and recast the vision. This step is necessary for each of the stages. Lay and pastoral leadership must walk the talk everywhere they go. Never underestimate inertia—it takes months, even years, of communication to accomplish the transformation. The best way to cast vision—and to retain our young people—is to live the vision.

Step Five: Develop permission-giving systems that empower people of all ages throughout the church. This gets harder with each succeeding stage. Transformation always involves mistakes. The question is, will the system reward or penalize people for making mistakes? Reduce committees and empower people to make decisions.

Step Six: Create short-term victories. Transforming a church takes much time, and people tend to lose their focus. "We can't do that," some will say. That kind of thinking ends transformation. Quick victories are needed if members are to persevere through the transformation process.

Step Seven: Constantly review and broaden support for the original vision. It is impossible to create enough short-term victories to keep the transformation process alive. This happens only when more and more people are being transformed and brought into the vision.

Step Eight: When experience shows that some of the ministries the church is fostering effectively reach and disciple new people, make these ministries into core ministries that will continue no matter who the pastor or lay leader may be. This is the most difficult of the last four steps of development. Many new attempts to reach out to the community will not work, but some will. Those that do work need to be funded and continued at all cost.

Step Nine: Become a learning church. A learning church is one in which people continually find new ways to improve effective ministries; one that considers new thoughts exciting and nurtures them; one in which permission-giving is the pattern; one that intentionally mentors young people as future leaders; one that considers mistakes to be opportunities; one in which people are constantly learning and experimenting together.

The role of church leadership, lay and pastoral, is to seek God's passion and vision continually; to revitalize the church by dispensing particular love to children and young people; to discover where He is working in their community and in their congregation and to join Him in finding people who need Jesus.

---

1. Donald W. Morgan, *Share the Dream, Build the Team* (Grand Rapids, Mich.: Baker Books, 2002), 13

2. Ron Crandall, *Turnaround Strategies for the Small Church* (Nashville: Abingdon Press, 1995), 32

3. Clark Morphew, "Survey: Methodists Want Docile Clergy," *The Beacon Journal* (Akron), July 31, 1993, A9, A10

4. Warren Bennis and Burt Nanus, *Leaders: The Strategies for Taking Charge* (New York: Harper & Row, 1985), 21.

5. Ibid.

CHAPTER 7

Developing a Child-Centered Ministry

by N. Jean Parchment

Norma Jean Parchment served as departmental director for women's, children's, and family ministries in the Ontario Conference. She currently resides in Laurel, Maryland.

Andrew came to visit. After his visit, my To Do list looked something like this:

- Get couch cushions from the bedroom (used to keep him from bumping into the wall).
- Replace all rubber tips on door stoppers (he delighted in removing them).
- Clean hand prints from patio door (he loved looking outside).
- Dispose of drowned plant that Andrew had watered (the hose was his favorite toy).
- Replace decorations on coffee table (they'd been unsafe for him).
- Replace kitchen rugs (he tripped on them).

Cleaning up after curious, active, adorable, strong-willed, intelligent, thirteen-month-old Andrew left, I reflected on all the changes we had made to our home to ensure a safe environment for him. It had been necessary to rearrange some rooms and alter our daily schedules, not always to our comfort, but we had given priority to what was best for this child. Every adult was on high alert for Andrew's safety and happiness. We each assumed the responsibility of getting down to his level to understand his needs and desires.

What made the entire experience of having this little visitor such a joy even when it entailed reorganizing significant areas of our everyday life? Love. A natural outgrowth of love is providing the best for him, and, at this developmental stage, that meant a child-centered environment.

The great news is that heaven is child-centered. Jesus gave us a glimpse of the atmosphere of heaven: "See that you do not look down on one of these little ones. For I tell you that their angels in heaven always see the face of my Father." "Let the little children come to me, and do not hinder them, for the kingdom of heaven belongs to such as these" (Matthew 18:10; 19:14, NIV).

There are two messages in these verses: 1. God and the angels are involved in active communication focusing on each child living on earth. 2. Heaven is 100 percent child-centered.

The Big Question

Can we imagine children, like Andrew in our house, running with excitement and awe from one room of a heavenly mansion to another, experiencing all that they could by touching all that can be touched, pulling and pushing anything that can be moved, banging things around, shouting, laughing, exclaiming, and praising God? Can we imagine them running through the parks, fields, and forests, riding the animals, climbing the trees, swinging over the streams, and jumping in and out of the water with the freedom of knowing they won't get hurt? How awesome! How exciting!

If heaven is child-centered and God and the angels focus on ministry to children, why are some of our churches hesitant to adopt this heavenly model? What if each administrator, each pastor, each elder, deacon, deaconess, and each member were to commit to making the church a happy, safe, and child-centered place? Is that a realistic wish? Is it practical?

What would the church look like, feel like, sound like if we took seriously Jesus' teaching that the kingdom of heaven belongs to the children? Could God be asking us to allow His church to become so child-centered that when the children come, they will experience a taste of the happiness and freedom of heaven?

Absence Is a Symptom

It was our first Sabbath in a large city church that my husband was asked to pastor. During the Sabbath School hour, as I scanned the pews of this very full church, I wondered, *Where are the young people?* The children's department was well attended, but the teens and young adults were just not visible. We soon discovered them visiting in the hallways and outside the church. When the eleven o'clock service started, they made their way to the balcony, forming a congregation all their own. Because the young people did not feel that the Sabbath School program was relevant, they simply did not attend.

I felt my mission needed to be focused on this mid-teen to young adult age group. Others who had a similar passion for the spiritual well-being of these young people began to work with me. However, there were obstacles. First, all the usable space was already occupied; it was impossible to find additional room for another class. Second, the majority of the church board were adamant against forming a specialized class. They claimed that the young people were old enough to integrate with the adults, and the program proposal that we submitted did not include the traditional lesson study, mission story, or Sabbath School program.

We had no apologies for the proposal. Realizing that many of these young people were facing challenges that were not being addressed by the current Sabbath School lessons or any other program of the church, we persisted in a nontraditional approach. It was our assumption that to be effective, we must be intentional, focusing on the felt needs.

Reluctantly, the church board gave permission for this specialized class to be held in the choir loft. We jumped at the opportunity.

To establish this group, we took the following steps:

- We enlisted the help of an elder who had history and rapport with this age group.
- We discovered the natural leaders among the young people, and made personal invitations to them, and enlisted their help in inviting their friends.
- We encouraged the young people to identify what they perceived as their needs.

The first Sabbath was very discouraging. Only a small number attended. Yet, having committed to ministry even if only one came, we continued with the program.

We began by explaining the purpose of the class. We emphasized that this was their group, not to be directed or monopolized by the adults. We would serve as sponsors, resource people, and liaisons. The young people were responsible for their program. They would choose discussion topics and the direction of the class as long as it pertained to their spiritual, emotional, or social well-being. Each young person who was comfortable doing so would have a turn leading out in the discussion and also in suggesting what would be discussed. Prayer for each other was an integral part of the service, and we were armed with Bibles as our frame of reference.

Word about what was happening in the choir loft spread like wildfire. To our joy, in a very short time, we were filled to capacity. The excitement grew. The group requested that we meet not only on Sabbath mornings, but also on Friday evenings and Sabbath afternoons. Excited about being in their own class, they invited their nonmember friends as well.

Currently, many of the class members are still enjoying church and serving in leadership capacities. One young lady who was a member of the group invited a classmate from public school. This young man became a member of the church and over time served in different leadership positions in the church, including the office of head elder. Eventually, he went to an Adventist college to study for the ministry.

I experienced the young people's concern for others as well. One Wednesday evening my doorbell rang. There stood four of the group members. "We came to have prayer with you," they announced.

What made the difference in these young people's attitude toward the church? They realized that their church cared about them. Its members were willing to reorganize and reprioritize in order to provide an arena of love and acceptance where their social, physical, emotional, and spiritual needs could be met. Church became relevant, relational, and happy.

A Wider Ministry

Years after experiencing this success with ministry to young people, I was asked to direct children's ministries at the conference level. Using as my frame of reference the principles learned with the youth group, I quickly formed a committee of individuals who were currently actively involved with ministry to children. I felt that the strength of a ministry must be based on an infrastructure that included the teachers and leaders in children's ministries.

The committee felt it most important that this ministry reflect the needs of the churches. Therefore, through questionnaires and needs assessments we asked, "What are your greatest needs?"

In response, a large percentage of leaders indicated the need for training in child development issues and practical hands-on information on how to meet the spiritual, physical, social, and emotional needs of children. These responses verified our belief that a large number of adults who have a heart for children and youth and who accept the task of ministering to them are not generally trained to do so. When faced with this challenge, many become fearful and apprehensive.

When leaders understand the principles of teaching and learning and the importance and how to's of forming relationships, the fear factor is lessened. This results in meaningful relationships between the generations. Children will be naturally drawn to these adults because they are understood and nurtured. And when parents are more aware of the spiritual, emotional, and social needs of their children and know how to fill these needs, they tend to be more involved in their children's everyday life, including their church life.

Churches that understand how to meet the needs of their younger members will not be afraid to feature family-inclusive ministry. They become places where worship and social activities involve the entire family, where children and youth become the backbone of the worship services rather than being patronized, entertained, or overlooked.

The strength of this ministry depends on two factors: the involvement of members of the local churches and their utilization of the resources available from the conference office. To move toward this ideal in our conference, we did the following:

- We surveyed children's ministries leaders in the local churches to discover the nature of their challenges and then provided workshops to meet these needs.
- We asked professionally trained teachers to give seminars/workshops on areas of their expertise.
- We requested individuals in the local churches who were making outstanding contributions to ministry to children to share their expertise with others through workshops.

We instituted an annual weekend leadership training program. The programming began early Friday afternoon; children's ministries coordinators attended a presentation designed specifically for them. A weekend program followed that included general presentations and multiple workshops addressing many areas of ministry.

Response to this leadership training program was overwhelmingly positive. Many churches ensured that their entire children's ministries staff would attend the weekend event. A resource video library was made available for isolated churches and for continual training throughout the year.

We've heard it said that the proof of the pudding is in the eating. The proof of the success of this program was determined by the positive difference it made in the churches. Churches began to realize the benefit of working toward being child-centered. One children's ministries coordinator commented, "These leadership programs made a difference to me both as a leader and as a parent. I've grown in understanding what child development is all about and the different needs of children. And I've been able to help my church become much more child-friendly."

Another church reported that when they became a child-centered church, their numbers increased. The children were so excited about their program that they insisted that the parents take them to Sabbath School on time. One parent asked to join the church because "this church meets the needs of my child."

With joy we celebrated the baptism of a young woman who, hearing about the leadership program, asked if she could take the courses. Through these courses she studied herself into the church and presently serves as a Cradle Roll teacher, bringing the love of Jesus to little children.

Our Goal

What does a happy, child-centered church look like? It's a church in which the leaders and members genuinely value the presence of each child and young person, not only in words but also in actions.

It's a church in which the pastor and lay leaders take seriously the words of Jesus, "Where your treasure is, there will your heart be also." Therefore the members provide adequate funds, proportionate to ministry in other areas, to empower effective, relevant ministry for children and young people.

It's a church in which the entire church body takes responsibility for ensuring the physical, emotional, social, and spiritual safety of each child and youth who enters the premises. Therefore, the members provide rooms for the children and youth that are attractive, neat, and clean, with adequate ventilation.

It's a church in which child-centered ministry naturally reaches out to the community. Why? Programs that are pertinent to today's families within the church are relevant and attractive to families outside the church. When the church becomes relevant to its members, reaching out to the community becomes a natural outgrowth of ministry.

A happy church is one that follows Jesus' model of ministry to children. Love motivated Jesus to say, "Let the little children come to me and don't stop them, because the kingdom belongs to such as these." And when love is our motivator, our attitude will be that of Christ, who *unsparingly* practices unconditional acceptance, affirmation, and encouragement. He has given us the privilege of making His church a happy place for each of our children and young people—a place bathed in an atmosphere of praise to God through the unconditional love each member models daily.

CHAPTER 8

Powerful Ways to Reach Youth

by Walter S. Rogers

Walter S. Rogers is the youth pastor of the Seventh-day Adventist church in Aldergrove, British Columbia. He says that while he likes hockey playoffs and sports cars, they'll be irrelevant a million years from now. That's why working with God to reach young people gets him excited.

Flying home for Christmas with my family requires that I know three things: where I am, where I want to go, and how I will get there. As a church we also need to know where we are and where we want to go, and then we need to find a way to get there. My hope and prayer is that our church will not only retain our young people and build them into passionate disciples of God, but that it will also reach many of those youth outside the church who are hurting and in desperate need of a Savior.

So, where are we? Overall in North America, our church is growing more slowly than the population at large. In other words, our church in North America is shrinking relative to the population. To say that is not the way it should be is an extreme understatement. Are you willing to sit back and wish somebody else would do something about it?

More to our point here, 40 to 50 percent of Adventist youth leave the church by their mid-twenties. These are young people who, by being baptized, have publicly said, "I want to follow Jesus for the rest of my life." More than half of them stay, and that's good. But we can do better.

Ask yourself why Coca Cola can sell sugar water all over the world while our church cannot even convince our own youth to stay connected to an incredible God. It makes no sense. God is relevant to every generation, every culture, at every time. If ever He does not appear to be, it's because we've misrepresented Him.

What is our goal? Is it to raise *nice kids* who attend church every week, read their Bibles every morning, and wait for marriage to have sex? These are all good things, but they could go through all these motions and still totally miss salvation. God wants people who passionately follow Him, who change the world around them for Him and cause major damage to Satan's territory. He wants people who aren't politically correct—who don't believe all religions are equal; people who get annoyed with bench warmers and pew sitters and are involved in real, powerful ministry; passionate disciples who keep Satan on the run.

If we are to drastically change the results of our ministry to young people—and so keep them connected to God—we need to drastically change our approach. If we tweak what we are currently doing, we will tweak what we are currently getting, and losing half our young people is not something I want to see tweaked! I want to see an about-face.

How to Get There

In my experience in youth ministry, I have found three things that have worked in powerful ways to reach youth.

1. The art of leadership. As John C. Maxwell has said, everything rises and falls on leadership. It takes leaders to bring about healthy change. Instead of reading about it, talking about it, and wishing somebody would do something about it, when leaders see a need, they meet it.

The critical part about leadership is that the first person they lead is themselves. As a leader, it's my responsibility to grow continually, to learn more about leadership every day. As I read books, magazine articles, and find leaders who will mentor me, my ministry can become more effective.

2. The understanding that kids need commitment and love more than they need coolness. They need role models with character and a passionate walk with God. The media gives them all the coolest role models possible, but those role models don't have characters worthy of imitation.

Researcher Roger Dudley wrote, "Over and over it is reported that the reason for leaving and staying away from the church is not doctrinal but relational."[1] Today's youth relate much better when God is described in relational terms and when doctrines are communicated in practical ways rather than focusing primarily in terms of logic and theory. So, let's find relevant ways to communicate our Bible truth to the next generation.

3. The realization that relevant and powerful ministry doesn't need to be complicated, but should actually be quite simple. A good friend once handed me a book named *The Secrets of the Simply Youth Ministry.* The title offended me a bit. I had spent the first few years of my ministry thinking that the bigger, more exciting, and better-rehearsed a program was, the better it was; the more orchestrated and organized my ministry was, the more effective it would be. But "simply youth ministry" just did not fit that paradigm. However, now that I've read the book, the stress level in my ministry has decreased by about half, because I now realize that effective ministry does not need to be complicated.

Simple Youth Ministry

Here are a few of the ways I have simplified my ministry and maintained, if not increased, my effectiveness:

1. I do not aim at having an incredibly dynamic ministry that attracts hundreds of youth. Nor do I work at producing a powerful program each week that brings kids to the front for tear-filled commitments. That can be exciting stuff, but I can very easily burn myself out striving for that and yet gain very little. My long-term goal is simply to help young people become mature Christian adults. It's so obvious. And it is bite-sized. This focus has led me to do programming in such a way that people are not attached to the program but to a personal relationship with God.

One of the problems with a ministry that consists of dynamic, exciting programs every week is that the young people graduate into a vacuum. Once they belonged to the program, but now they're too old for it, and because they're not yet attached to the adult church, they leave. I want the children and youth in my church to be attached to God and serve Him, all the while realizing that the church is one of the best places in which to do that. Awesome programs can be a tool to bring youth closer to God, but they can never substitute for closeness with God.

Building mature, adult Christians means running a program for kids that gets them excited about God and His church. Then, as they go through their teen years, we must mentor them into service and leadership positions. By the time they graduate from high school, leaving church is not really an option because they are running a significant part of it!

2. Simplifying my ministries has included harnessing social energy. Ever walk into a meeting where you spot a friend you have not seen for about three weeks? You find it hard to focus on the program. So often our teaching, whether academic or spiritual, fights social energy. We want those in the audience to sit still and listen to the program. What if instead of fighting this social energy we tried to harness it?

Sabbath School is supposed to be interactive, but often three or four individuals dominate the discussion. It's true that people can visit in the church foyer before and after the main service, but why not simply make interaction more central to our programming strategy? Make the leader more of a facilitator than an instructor. For example, I divide those attending youth Sabbath School into groups of four, give them a list of Bible passages about some topic, and ask them to be prepared to summarize their conclusions when the time is up. If I tried to push my own opinion on the topic, most of the youth would turn their brains off. Instead, they'll compare and contrast each group's opinions in relation to the verses they've just read.

If my teens want a weekly, exciting, dynamic program, they'll have to run it. I will be there to support and coach them, help them with funding and other things, but I will not do a huge program for them. Let me explain. I have sat through some very exciting (and loud) youth programs in which the youth participated halfheartedly and which afterwards they criticized and complained about. At first I was in shock. I thought that what we had given them—dim lights, loud music, lyrics on PowerPoint, and free food—was exactly what they wanted. The problem is that no matter how good the program is, if it's run by the adults, it will almost never be good enough.* Now, instead, I more often do a

---

*I've found this to be true of regularly scheduled programs, either weekly, bi-weekly or monthly. With youth retreats and other quarterly to annual events, there is much more time to prepare, and they are rare enough that the "novelty" does not so easily wear off.

program with interactive, learner-based activities. Samples of a couple such programs follow.

A children's Sabbath School program (KIDS Zone): Before the kids arrive, we've prepared the room with several game stations (Legos, Bible board games, etc.), and staff are ready to play so that kids who are early can build relationships with staff and others and not get bored. The program starts with fifteen minutes of interactive games, from "duck-duck-goose" to "statues." This time breaks down social inhibitions, gets the kids laughing and having fun, and, especially important, makes visitors feel welcome and gives them the opportunity to interact with others in a very informal way.

Next, we have a fifteen-minute song service that goes from fast-paced action songs to meaningful worship songs. (I often remind the children that songs are a gift we are singing to God; He is our audience during our worship time.) Fifteen minutes of visual-based teaching follows, including object lessons, skits, and stories. Since kids are such concrete thinkers, many concrete examples and visual props are needed to illustrate every major point.

KIDS Zone concludes with a fifteen-minute review of the Sabbath School lesson. Groups of three to six kids per staff member discuss what the lesson teaches and how they can apply it to their lives. Too often we teach kids the theory, but neglect to teach how it actually changes real life.

Youth Sabbath School: We start with a few interactive games that get the kids out of their seats and moving around.* Then they are divided into small groups of four or five and study either a chapter of the Bible or several passages on a single topic. Everyone gets a chance to read, to share how the reading applies (or doesn't apply) to their lives, and to ask questions. After about twenty minutes of this we gather everyone together and discuss what each group found. We close with prayer.

---

*For example a list of ten "would you rather _____," "have you ever _____" type questions regarding which kids have to vote with their feet and go to one side of the room or the other depending on their answer.

Although it is important that the leaders research the topic or passages so they are prepared to handle questions that arise, it's best to encourage feedback and suggestions from the students.

"Christian Café": To provide a fun place to hang out, a place to which kids can bring non-Christian friends who would not be ready to attend a traditional church service, we have started a "Christian Café" on Friday nights. The youth and staff redecorate the Sabbath School room to resemble a coffee shop. Since lighting comes from lava lamps, candles, and Christmas lights, the room is quite dim, with a relaxing atmosphere. We play high-quality contemporary Christian music and just hang out for the first bit. We provide snacks, and large sheets of paper tacked to a wall give those attending a place to draw and paint. Later, a youth, a youth leader, or pastor provides a short devotional message, and then we do fun stuff like Bible Improv (similar to the show *Who's Line Is It Anyway?* but on biblical themes).

Small-group Bible study: The most meaningful program I am involved with is probably the simplest of them all. Even though it has been around for thousands of years, I doubt there will ever be anything more effective for developing spiritual maturity. I'm talking about small peer-group Bible studies. During the week a group of three to six young adults read the same ten to fifteen chapters for devotions. Then we meet on Sunday nights at a Tim Horten's or McDonald's or a similar place and talk about which verses spoke to us, what questions we have, how this passage applies to us, and how God is leading in our lives.

We keep casually inviting friends to join, and when our group reaches about six people, we divide into two groups. We do this because we have a foundational value that everyone present gets to contribute significantly to the conversation. I have seen too many Sabbath Schools where two or three vocal people dominate the discussion while many others sit there and watch or stare off into space. When you limit the group to six or fewer, everyone can easily get involved and the group benefits by learning from everyone there. It would seem weird if someone were to sit there and not contribute.

If I were to say that this ministry has caught like wild fire in my church, I would be lying. Establishing it requires discipline and commitment; it's easy to find excuses not to do your devotions or show up for the Bible study. To succeed, you simply have to make it what it should be: a sacred commitment of time to grow closer to God. I have found that as I remain committed to casually inviting other people, they join as the Holy Spirit bugs them. Often, months pass between the initial invitation and their first visit. However, everyone who joins says that they really enjoy it and that it is a real blessing to them— especially the experience of personal Bible study and community.

I've learned an important lesson both from seminars I've attended and from my own experimentation with small-group curriculums: Small groups that are based on a program or some other outside resource seem to depend on the leader. The others in the group tend to come with the mind-set of "I wonder what Walter came up with this week?" I find that the best Bible studies are based directly on the Bible and on the insights brought by those attending. Like other learner-based, interactive ministries that I am experimenting with, it is less work for the leader, yet more effective.

After studying all sorts of ministry and leadership ideas, I've realized that no one really has it all together. None of the best ministers I know have it all together. God is the only One who has it all together—that's why we worship Him. Our job is comparable to that of the children of Israel crossing the Jordan: We have to let God handle the big challenges and do what we can by stepping out in faith. We have to rely on God to change lives in ways that we cannot.

So don't sit on the border of the Promised Land and stare at the giants we face as a church, despairing because they're too big for us. Of course they are; but they're not too big for God. Do whatever you can with the power of God to reach out to the youth of your church. Learn all you can about leadership so that God can use you more effectively. Use these ideas or anyone else's and adapt them to fit your local situation. Let your youth come up with their own ideas.

You do the possible and watch God do the impossible.

---

1. Roger L. Dudley, *Why Our Teenagers Leave the Church* (Hagerstown, Md.: Review and Herald, 2000), 99.

CHAPTER 9

Heaven on Earth Every Week

by Aileen Andres Sox

Aileen Andres Sox, editor of Our Little® Friend *and* Primary Treasure® *at Pacific Press® Publishing Association, Nampa, Idaho, believes each Seventh-day Adventist church should be "heaven on earth" for those who attend. Sabbath mornings find her at the Kuna, Idaho, Adventist church.*

When I travel around the country teaching various children's ministries seminars, I make a startling promise: "If you pay attention to children, your church will grow—I guarantee it." I don't make this claim lightly; I make it because of my experience in my own church. In the past fourteen years, and most especially in the past six, my church has experienced explosive growth.

Kuna, some ten miles from Boise, Idaho, used to be a small farming community. These days, along with everything else in the Treasure Valley, Kuna is booming. Subdivisions are sprouting like mushrooms in fields that once grew alfalfa or sugar beets. And Kuna is within easy driving distance of *five* nearly brand-new Wal-Mart Super Centers—a sure sign of a growing community, because Wal-Mart's corporate strategy targets such places.

At the time I joined the Kuna church in 1988, there were fewer than twenty active families. In those early days we had only a few children in Sabbath School—one of the signs to me of a church that isn't thriving. But the warmth and conviviality of the congregation drew me, even though the church was suffering, as do all small churches, with too much to do and too few people to do it.

Now we have eighty-five active families, with some one hundred kids under the age of eighteen! It's a church where, if you're fifty or more, you're older than 75 percent of the congregation. (I figured that out on a recent birthday. Sigh . . .)

The people in my church have taught me things about God's love that I doubt I could have learned in any other way. They place enormous emphasis on prayer and put their confidence in God's love-filled answers. Their joy in one another and in coming together to worship makes each Sabbath heaven on earth for me. And I really, truly anticipate living on Kuna (say *Cue-na,* not *Coo-na*) Street in the New Jerusalem.

Are we perfect? No. We're all too human and live in this world, after all. I'm sure there isn't a heartache out there that we haven't experienced in some way. Our interactions with people can sometimes be impulsive, petty, selfish, and lacking in gratitude. Sometimes we whine instead of digging in and making what difference we can.

Is our way of "doing church" for everyone? No. Our style is informal and can appear disorganized. We'll probably always run a little late, a little long, and a whole lot casual on Sabbath morning. Some of us will never show up for church committees because the drive is too far and the kids need to be in bed and our lives are way too frantic. The bulletin probably never will accurately reflect the actual participants because our lives are busy and last-minute changes have to be made in the morning worship schedule—even if it's only because a weekend in the mountains suddenly had more appeal!

Paying Attention to Kids

But for the Kuna church, that stuff is small stuff. We get the big stuff right. We can always count on a big turnout for baby showers, baptisms, weddings, graduations, school programs, and Pathfinder Sabbath. The annual pie auction to raise money for the Pathfinders can turn $200 worth of stuff into nearly $1,000 for the club—yet leave no one feeling bad because they can spend no more than $20.

Our church is full of small-business owners, many of whom hire Kuna kids as part-time help. Our first Vacation Bible School in a number of years attracted a hundred children and more than fifty volunteers! A number of Kuna church children attend church school only because generous members subsidize their entire tuition. In addition, the church subsidizes part of the tuition of every Kuna child going to any church school in the area. I've never once heard anyone complain about spending money for Sabbath School furniture or supplies or Vacation Bible School this past year. The attitude is always, "We'll find a way." A special offering brought in some $700 for VBS—one of the "ways" Kuna found.

We applaud kids. Most of us would prefer *more* involvement by kids in our services rather than less, and we have a lot of participation now. Children participate in the service by reading the morning's Scripture passage, singing or playing special music, and singing in a children's praise team. Junior deacons and deaconesses have assignments whenever their adult counterpart-mentors do. Kids greet at the front door along with their parents or older siblings. Kids' achievements—honor roll, graduation, awards—are reported and applauded during praise or announcement time. Their prayer requests are taken to God's throne just as certainly as are the adults' prayers. Our children's offering is the bulkiest cash offering each Sabbath morning. Who can resist those cute little kids, each having a basket that he or she wants you to put something in? Each year the nominating committee works first on the positions for children's Sabbath Schools. And we pick the best story-tellers we have for the weekly children's story.

We don't mind the noise generated by children during a worship service. We hold our worship service first and Sabbath School second because we know doing so helps children endure better. We provide "busy" bags for each child under age ten or so and are looking to purchase about twenty booster seats this year to help kids ages two to six see better and thus be less restless during the service. (Go to www.churchchairs4kids.com to learn more.) We encourage parents of young children to use wireless headsets from our sound system to listen to the sermon while walking their restless children throughout our facility.

It has become a tradition to give each Kuna kid a book from Pacific Press or the Review and Herald for Christmas, each dedicated baby a toddler's worship book, and each person baptized a Bible. When a baby is born, our pastor visits the hospital with a copy of Kay Kuzma's *Preparing for Your Baby's Dedication: A Guide for Parents,* because we want parents to know right from the beginning their church will participate in their child's spiritual life.

Kuna is a demonstrative church family. People who want hugs can always find them here. I've learned that our teens and college kids especially seem to appreciate physical affection. Since I'm old enough to be their (very young!) grandma, I take advantage of that and hug each one I see. At first they don't know quite how to take it, but pretty soon if I don't hug them, they seek me out and say they want their hug.

Making It Personal

I discovered a few years ago that none of the teens were taking *Insight* magazine when it was provided for them in Sabbath School. Since I order the various Sabbath School publications, I cancelled the *Insight* subscriptions. Parents complained. (I should have talked with them first, by the way.) I told them why I had cancelled the magazine, but got to thinking about the problem and began investigating. I finally concluded that the teens were leaving the magazine behind either because of some peer pressure thing or else because they thought only "kids" took papers home. I discovered that *Insight* could be sent to each home for mere pennies more than getting it in bulk at the church. So I collected addresses and had it mailed to each teen's home.

Now I call each home once a year to see if the magazine is being read. If it is, we gladly renew it. Eventually, of course, the kids outgrow the magazine, but sending it home has the terrific extra benefit of it always being available, even if the teen doesn't attend church on any given week. This happens frequently around here since we have an academy in the area that draws a lot of kids for various weekend events.

Gary Smalley came to this area to give a marriage seminar. Because of generous donations from several businesses in the community, it was a free event. I first heard the news on the Treasure Valley's award-winning Christian radio station, KTSY, which also happens to be owned by the Idaho Conference of Seventh-day Adventists. I immediately called my pastor to tell him about Gary Smalley so that we could procure tickets to be sure we had enough for any couple who wanted to go. Pastor John not only did that, he also volunteered to take care of each couple's children at the church that day. He planned a whole day for the kids—from a church service about dinosaurs and creation to a picnic-style lunch and an afternoon of activities that kept them interested and happy until their parents came to pick them up.

We've also entertained children for a parents' night out on a Saturday evening. A parents' night out right before Christmas would be a wonderful gift for those who need to shop without children around. (Some churches have a weekly family night that includes a meal for one or two dollars per person, followed by Pathfinders, parenting or other seminars, and childcare. The evening ends promptly so that kids can get to bed on time.)

One Sabbath a few months ago, before the church service started, I noticed that a mother and her two young children were attending for the first time. Almost the first question the mother asked me after we introduced ourselves was, "What kind of Sabbath Schools do you have?" I assured her that Kuna Sabbath Schools were terrific. (I'm only a little prejudiced!) Another young family mentioned to me that the reason they picked Kuna was because people noticed their kids and remembered their names, because people asked them how they were and cared about the answer, and because several invited them home to eat. And a young father told me recently, "It's really stressful to be in a place where a kid's noise seems to bother everyone. At Kuna they make noise and no one cares."*

I have learned that parents almost always want to go to a church where their kids will be happy. That's why I say that paying attention to kids results pretty inevitably in church growth.

---

*Encouraging parents to sit with their children in the *front* pews instead of in the back can make a world of difference. If kids can see, they behave better—that's why booster seats are a good idea.

Gary Hopkins's comments:

Consider creating your church as a community. Research by Roberts and colleagues on "school as a community" is powerful and may have implications for churches as communities. When students had a high perception of their school as a community, they tended to read more outside of school, enjoyed reading more, enjoyed class more, liked school more, avoided work less, were more academically motivated, trusted and respected school more, enjoyed helping others learn more, and had higher educational aspirations and expectations. Academically, they performed higher on reading and math achievement tests. And they had more concern for others and higher self-esteem and resolved conflicts better.

When teachers had a high perception of their school as a community, they had higher expectations for student learning, trusted students more, enjoyed teaching more, were more satisfied with teaching, and had a higher overall satisfaction with their job. When the school was rated as having a high sense of community, the principal was more competent and supportive, parents were more supportive, and there were more positive teacher-student relations.

Though no research on church as community has been reported, the findings noted above excite the imagination regarding the potential power of this concept in our churches!

See: W. Roberts; A. Hom; and V. Battistich, "Assessing Students' and Teachers' Sense of the School as a Caring Community." (Paper presented at the American Educational Research Association, April 1995.)

Ministry to Children

CHAPTER 10

Start by Learning Their Names

by Ron and Karen Flowers

Ron and Karen Flowers are directors of the Department of Family Ministries at the General Conference of Seventh-day Adventists, Silver Spring, Maryland. This chapter is adapted from an article in Ministry *magazine, November 2000. Used by permission.*

It's amazing how much difference something as simple as knowing someone's name can make. A friend of mine who goes to a rather large church told me a story. It's easy for a kid to get lost in a big church, particularly a kid who goes to public school or doesn't particularly shine. My friend discovered a young girl in her large congregation who had the same name as her daughter. She introduced herself to the girl; showed her a picture of her daughter, now grown and moved away; and told her that seeing her in church and knowing she shared a name with her daughter made her think warm thoughts about her family.

After that, my friend made a special point of connecting with her daughter's "namesake" every Sabbath. The girl struggled through adolescence and had a baby before she was married. But week by week my friend was there with a friendly smile and an encouraging word. Adolescence is behind the girl now. She is married, and she is also still in church. Her bond with my friend remains. It started with just a name.

Last week we were back in our pew in our local church after nearly two months of work-related travel. Karen, along with a team of five other people, is responsible for the children's story each week, so all the children are her friends. During the worship hour, as the children go to the front for their story time, they collect offerings for Christian education. As Karen offered a dollar bill to a favorite three-year-old passing by, he stopped dead in his tracks and put his hand on his hips. Squinting and scrunching up his nose as if he were unable to be completely sure, he inquired, "Are you Grandma?"

Now, we have no biological grandchildren, though we've "adopted" many. But Karen responded, "Why, yes! I haven't seen you for a long time."

"Well," he announced, lest she may have forgotten, "I'm Andrew." And with that he took the dollar and moved along.

Is our evaluation of the importance of knowing kids' names based merely on anecdotes? Actually, we have it on very good authority. In 1997 the National Longitudinal Study of Adolescent Health (AdHealth) collected data from ninety thousand American teens and eighteen thousand of their parents. This study provides a suitable capstone to the growing body of research that identifies the factors that predispose today's children and youth to involvement in high-risk behaviors and those factors that are most likely to protect them from harm. The one word that encapsulates all this research is *connectedness*. In short, kids who feel connected to family, church, school, and community are far less likely to participate in behaviors that put them at risk.[1]

Keep Kids Connected

What makes kids feel connected? Remembering that Susie has a biology test today and promising to pray for her. Taking time for fun. Opening one's home to kids. Setting sensible limits while maintaining reasonable flexibility. Being available. Asking questions that show interest in kids' lives and pursuits. Noticing a job well done. Treating kids fairly and equitably. Setting high expectations and communicating clearly one's disapproval of risky behaviors. Becoming a reliable source of good information. Listening with undivided attention. Watching out for the vulnerable.

Doctors Gary Hopkins and Bruce Heischober, physicians at Loma Linda University with expertise in youth at-risk behavior, wrote a seminar for parents on building connections that make a difference in the lives of children and youth.[2] Here is their bottom line: Connectedness takes time and requires genuine interest in young people and their issues. It means going where the kids are. It involves dialogue—listening as well as talking. Connectedness is about warmth and caring and love and friendship. It is also about supervision and setting limits. It's about building trust and holding on during the hard times.

Connectedness is about mentoring and making wholesome values attractive. It requires a willingness to negotiate and to release responsibility to young people in keeping with their growing maturity. Connectedness is about getting involved and giving of oneself. It is about looking out for kids who are discouraged or troubled. Connectedness is about helping someone who has made a mistake to begin again. Connectedness is about supporting parents and families. It means opening one's family to include others in the circle of caring and fun. Connectedness is about becoming community.

But it can't happen until people like us start learning names.

---

1. R. W. Blum and P. M. Rinehard, *Reducing the Risk: Connections That Make a Difference in the Lives of Youth* (Minneapolis: Division of General Pediatrics and Adolescent Health, University of Minnesota, n.d.).

2. G. L. Hopkins; B. Heischober; and K. Flowers, "Connections That Make a Difference: Risk-Proofing Youth in a High-Risk Society," *Family Ministries Planbook: Facing Family Crises* (Silver Spring, Md.: Department of Family Ministeries, General Conference of Seventh-day Adventists, 1999), 45–62.

Gary Hopkins's comments:

Resneck and colleagues report that "regardless of the number of parents in the household, whether families were rich or poor, regardless of race and ethnicity, children who reported feeling connected to a parent are protected against many different kinds of risks including emotional distress; suicidal thoughts and attempts; cigarette, alcohol, and marijuana use; violent behavior; and early sexual activity."

When these same students felt a high sense of connectedness at school, they were involved in fewer violent acts, were protected from cigarette, alcohol, and marijuana use, and delayed first sexual intercourse. Overall, school connectedness was consistently associated with healthier behaviors and better health among students.

Connectedness implies relationships.

See: M. D. Resnick; P. S. Bearman; R. W. Blum; K. E. Bauman; K. M. Harris; J. Jones; J. Tabor; T. Beuhring; R. E. Sieving; M. Shew; M. Ireland; L. H. Bearinger; J. Udry, "Protecting Adolescents From Harm: Findings From the National Longitudinal Study on Adolescent Health." *Journal of the American Medical Association,* 278(10):823–832.

Treat Them As If They're Important

by Willie and Elaine Oliver

Willie Oliver is director of family ministries in the North American Division of the Seventh-day Adventist Church, and Elaine Oliver is director of financial aid at Columbia Union College and family consultant for the church in North America. Myrna Tetz interviewed them.

MT: Willie, soon after you returned from presenting a Family Friendly Church seminar, you told me about a man who had asked, "How can we keep children quiet during church?" You said that you were disturbed because in Sabbath School the children hear stories, put things on the flannel board, sing songs with motions, then, during church, they're supposed to sit absolutely quiet for over an hour. I caught your passion and later, that of your wife. That conversation led to the publishing of this book. Did your early ministry include a ministry for children?

WO: My ministry began in New York City; I was youth pastor of a 700-member church in the Bronx. There were kids of all ages in this church, and I was involved with youth leaders and other people who worked with the children and youth in designing and developing programs and activities. Then I became senior pastor of a church not far away, a church that grew out of this mother church during evangelistic meetings. The church was very small—about one hundred members on the books, but about thirty attending. We had Sabbath School, but no other youth program and very little on Sabbath afternoon for young people.

At the larger church I had helped develop a youth federation in the Bronx for the Greater New York Conference youth. So, when I became pastor of the smaller church, I engaged the federation's help to build the youth ministry of this smaller church. I'd been at that church just over a year when Elaine and I were married. By that time we had a youth ministry going—Sabbath School, afternoon meetings, and service activities. We also had young people coming to the prayer meeting service. Elaine helped me restructure the Sabbath School and build a strong ministry from the fledgling program that was there when she arrived.

MT: What were you doing when the North American Division asked you to be a part of the ministry there?

WO: At the time the North American Division asked me to work in the Family Ministries department, I was serving as Youth Ministries director (which included Pathfinders and Adventurers). Before that, I had been the director of Youth Ministries in the Greater New York Conference.

My dad passed on this youth ministry legacy. He was the kind of pastor who felt that church and spiritual activities meant way more than just attending church services. He involved young people in ministry and took them out into nature to enjoy God's world and helped them to understand that being a Christian doesn't mean being bored. While he had lots of churches, he always made time for our family, made the church into family time, because, as children, we were very involved with the church program.

MT: Elaine, what is your specific commitment to the children of the church?

EO: I was raised by my grandmother. She used to teach Sabbath School, and everyone loved going to her Sabbath School class. I enjoyed helping my grandmother prepare for Sabbath School, and I think that's where I developed this passion, this interest in working with children. Eventually, I started teaching Primary Sabbath School because that's an age I loved working with. They are old enough to sit still and be really involved. I continued my involvement in children's divisions right through my college years.

MT: What was your vision for youth and for the adults in your church?

EO: I never thought I would marry a minister—never thought that my Sabbath School involvement would lead into being a pastor's wife. Young families started coming to Willie's little church, and they brought their friends and neighbors, so we soon had a large group of children every Sabbath. I just naturally started planning a program for these kids.

My thinking about including the children in the church service started when I was very young. I never felt I was really a part of the church service. I always looked forward to going to Sabbath School but not necessarily church. I always loved the children's story on the few occasions when we had one. We started children's stories in our church service so that children had a reason to be part of it. The kids just loved being there. They appreciated having us, and we appreciated them—they became our children.

WO: When I came to that little church in the Bronx there were very few children, and they always looked bored. When Elaine started working in the children's divisions, the church began to flourish. At first, children were coming without their parents, but then the parents started coming to church—both members of our church who had quit coming to our services and members of other churches who had dropped out. There were many baptisms.

EO: It reminds me of the text in the Bible that says, "A child will lead them." I think that's one reason why ministry to children is so important—children are so innocent, so pure, and they have no ulterior motives. If we can get children to begin to understand the love of

Christ and to understand what this whole message is about, then perhaps the adults will be affected.

WO: There's something that I need to say at this juncture. As a little kid in church I always knew that my dad, the pastor, had great regard for the children. He was the one to tell the children's story and always included children in the worship service. And what was really moving to me was my dad preaching about people being ready for the Lord to come. He always said that the Lord is going to ask about the flock He gave us. Then Dad would say how much he wanted to see everyone in heaven and would call out his children's names: Oscar, Willie, Lila, Marcia, and Lettie. He said, "A church for children is a church that has a future." He often mentioned that he reveled in the fact that there were children in his churches. He said that meant those churches were alive, they had a future, and they wouldn't be dying off any time soon. He said that any place where children were present had life and a future. It made a real impression on me that children were important and that dad considered us, his children, important.

MT: Willie, what is your specific commitment as the director of Family Ministries?

WO: As director of Family Ministries, I work closely with Noelene Johnsson, director of Children's Ministries for the North American Division, in children's ministry. Right now we have a great passion for marriages. We think if we can help build strong, healthy marriages, we can build strong healthy families. When you have a strong marriage, you have a strong and healthy context for discipling children. When, on the other hand, people begin to lose hope in their marriages and stop coming to church, there's a lot of tension in the family. Then children begin to feel insecure and tend to start dropping out of church as well.*

---

*See the *Family Friendly Church* video available from Advent Source (ph. 800-328-0525).

This is not to say, by the way, that we're not interested in single parents. We certainly are, and we do workshops to enhance what single parents do with their children.

MT: Willie and Elaine, how do you see your vision for children and adults being accomplished?

WO: Parents, especially fathers, stand in the place of God. Children tend to view God in the same way they view their fathers—at least that's what the literature tells us. And most people come to God between the ages of five and thirteen. The more the adult membership will communicate to the children that they are loved, that they belong, the more that they are affirmed and highlighted in the worship service, the more they will feel connected and important in the church environment.

EO: One of the things that we can do is to get this important message passed on to everyone who sits on a church board. Oftentimes this is where decisions are being made—whether we are going to fix up the children's Sabbath School rooms, for instance. Is the money going somewhere else or to the children's programs? I know that often when churches are looking at scaling down the worship service, the first thing they take out is the children's story. If there's something extra that day and the time frame is tight, the children's story is the first to go. How do we stay committed and understand that, no, that should be the *last* thing to go? We can get rid of an extra song, maybe, or something else, but not the children's story.

You know, children are like automatons. They come to Sabbath School and church, and they have it all programmed in their brains as to what's going to happen; they know exactly when it's their time. We have to begin looking at our commitment to children through different lenses—how do we involve the whole family, and especially children, in the church service?

WO: Since children don't pay tithe, they comprise a constituency that isn't catered to. We must become intentional about serving children, making sure their needs are met, affirming them in the church. Otherwise, we'll tend to give them just the scraps, what's left over. I think it's important that we develop a church "lifestyle" of looking out for the children, realizing that if we lose them between five and thirteen, we may have lost them forever. We can't afford that. One of the best avenues to church growth is making sure that the children who are born into the church family are being nurtured and made to feel welcome so they'll want to remain in the church family.

MT: Elaine, in the Family Friendly Video you describe the inclusion of drama by young people that relates to the sermon by young people. Please describe this ministry.

EO: Drama is an incredible thing. At our church we include both a drama time and the children's story. We like both because we gear the drama more toward the adolescents and teens and anyone older than that. Having drama in the service takes a little bit of planning. The drama team has to find out what the pastor is going to speak about. Then they develop a three-to-five-minute skit portraying the main point of the sermon. It doesn't have to be anything formal. In a lot of churches people can be found to help because it's their way of being involved. It's a gift; there are people who have the gift of drama.

We've called our drama segments "Sermon Illumination," because there are people who felt uncomfortable with the word *drama*. Those times when we had to leave out the drama segment the adults asked, "Why have you stopped doing the Sermon Illumination?" Some people are visual learners. The drama segment draws their attention to the service and prepares them for what is coming in the sermon. And the younger children can relate to it too. If you have a children's story and a drama, you are keeping the children's attention for quite some time. I don't think in most places where it's done people have gotten flack for it. If you have the support of the pastor and board, then it goes pretty well. But you need to keep it to a minimum, time-wise—no fifteen-minute soap operas. There are so many biblical skits that are prepackaged; you can almost always find something that will fit your pastor's sermon.

WO: The Sermon Illumination is short, and because it's in story form, you communicate the point of the sermon material. So even if the pastor gets a little long-winded or talks above the children's heads, they get the point. We want to be intentional about reaching children every Sabbath morning so the worship service becomes an integral part of their lives and they don't just check out when the sermon begins.

MT: Describe your commitment to learning the names of children and adults in the churches you attend and the ones you visit.

WO: For me it has always been a matter of connecting with people. As a youth director, I was intentional about learning the names of the kids throughout the conference. Of course, I heard my dad saying it as well—that people consider nothing sweeter than hearing their own name. Knowing people's names brings them closer to you and brings others to you because they want to be sure that you know their names as well. Even adults are pulled in and feel regarded and respected and feel a sense of belonging when people know their names.

EO: I go out of my way to learn the children's names, though unfortunately I don't have the gift of remembering names like Willie does. Learning their names and finding out what is happening in their lives is important. I call them by name and ask them, "How is school going?" "How was your week?" Oftentimes teens think we adults are there to criticize them. Imagine if all the adults took it upon themselves to try and understand what's going on in their lives. They'd be amazed at what they'd find out. It means so much when someone knows your name—it melts you and makes a big difference.

MT: Are there people who have inspired you with their ministry to children and young people?

EO: I think specifically of a woman who was such an inspiration to me. She taught the kindergarten Sabbath School for years, probably decades. Because she had both money and a passion for children, she donated a lot of equipment. She started leading in Sabbath School when her children were young and continued even after they were grown. She really inspired me with her commitment to the children, her beautiful Sabbath School room, and how passionate she was about making Sabbath School a place of joy for young children.

WO: I think of a woman at our current church who has mentored junior ushers. She seats them in places where they feel important, dresses them in uniform, and has them usher people out at the end of the service. You can tell that these kids have been pulled into the church life. Sociologists have developed a theory on the notion of mattering, studying where people feel that they matter and where they feel marginalized. Where people think they matter, they do their best— they feel they can participate, they communicate, they are ready and willing to be involved in whatever is asked of them. Where people feel marginalized, they just hang back. They don't want to be there because they are not regarded or respected.

MT: How do you include your children in your ministry?

EO: We use them as guinea pigs. If we're writing something, we give it to them to proofread and we ask their opinions: "What do you think about this?" "Do you think it will be received well by kids your age?" And they'll tell us! They'll say, "Oh, no, that sounds too preachy. You might want to say such-and-such; you might want to change this word." They're very good at being our mentors, especially for adolescents. We try to include them as much as we can so they don't feel this ministry is working against them.

WO: By the way, they're not the up-front kind of kids. But sometimes they've come to our workshops, listened to what we are saying, spoken to some of the kids. When we're talking about children, if our children don't seem well adjusted or they don't seem involved, we wouldn't be as credible. We have goals and aspirations, and one is to be a loving family, to listen to one another, and to realize that the reason families exist is so that we can communicate the love of God to people.

Not that we're a perfect family, because we're not. We have our issues that we are constantly dealing with. There comes a time when children have to make their own choices. One parent told me only one of her four kids is still in the church, and one is a drug addict—even though she had worked hard to put her kids through our schools. Even when we do our best, our kids may not react in a positive way. That doesn't mean that we are failures.

MT: Any ideas for other parents on how to bring spirituality close to their children and young people?

WO: The ValuGenesis research taught us that family worship accomplishes the most when every member of the family takes the lead. We have different members of the family lead out in family worship. Both kids come to our bedroom in the morning. We read a devotional and talk about prayer requests and other things. When Elaine reads, Julian leads the family in calling for prayer requests and praises, and then he also prays. When Jessica does the reading, I do the requests for prayer and praise and I pray, and so on. It's a time when we can come together as a family. We talk about the love of God and how He has promised that He will take care of us and even if He doesn't, there's a purpose for our life.

Keep it real. We emphasize that it is important to be with the community of believers. However, there are times when we take a family outing on a Sabbath. Or we may stay home and have praise and worship. Or go to the beach, recognizing that God is everywhere. We talk with our children about how they can make a difference in someone's life today. About being kind to the person being picked on. We try to be practical with them. We talk about how, even in troubled times, we can have peace. During the sniper hunt in our area, our daughter praised God because she was still safe and her friends were safe.

We talk about how we have to live our lives according to God's will and purpose. We read something and ask, "What would Jesus do?" We say that we should ask that question every time we have a decision to make. Since we started asking that, it's become second nature. We've stressed that it's OK to ask forgiveness. If we've yelled at them or issued discipline that wasn't fair, we ask forgiveness.

EO: We just try to make Christianity very real. We've learned a lot from our children—they've been raising us!

CHAPTER 12

Intentional Children's Ministry

by Victoria D. Harrison

Victoria Harrison, children's ministries pastor of Community Praise Center in Alexandria, Virginia, is pursuing a doctorate in ministry with an emphasis in family life. Her passion is introducing families, including children, to Jesus for renewal, healing, and discipleship.

I guess, the truth be told, I am not that interested in "changing the statistics," at least not as a first priority. For many decades we have used numbers as a key measure of our success. We look for the big producers of baptisms and measure our effectiveness by mass. Have we unintentionally overlooked something?

We had just read Scripture at a Wednesday evening children's Bible study class, and were presenting the Sabbath from Creation to now. Lissy's* hand shot up, and her mouth opened in tandem, "You mean God clears His calendar every Sabbath just hoping that we will spend the time with Him? What if I don't choose to spend time with Him, does He mow the lawn or start a new choir to fill up His day?"

When the giggles died down, we clarified that God does indeed clear His calendar just hoping we will want to become better acquainted with Him.

"I get it, I get it," gasped Ashanti breathlessly. "We keep the Sabbath because God wants us to be a friend. That means we have to spend time with Him, because friends talk all the time."

Then the conversation crescendoed: "I thought we keep Sabbath because God is gonna be mad if we don't." "Really, God made Sabbath

---

*All the names used in this chapter have been changed.

so we can do stuff together—stuff we both like." "Yeah, if we spend time with Jesus and don't let other junk get in the way, God will say we are faithful and everyone will know He's the winner!"

In our efforts to get decisions and assure conformity to the twenty-seven fundamentals of the church, we have sometimes overlooked that the doctrinal position of all believers, including children, must be underpinned by a relationship with Christ.

An analogy might be of a man and woman who agree to marry. They dress up for the occasion, show up on time, recite the marriage vows, and are introduced to the congregation as husband and wife. But after the certificate is filed with the county, they choose to live in separate countries. Their communication consists of calls on birthdays and holidays and when they're preparing their taxes. Yes, the couple has followed all the protocols, but they're missing the real intent of marriage: companionship, growth, relationship.

Today's challenge is broader than just decisions and baptisms; it includes the foundations for companionship, growth, and relationship with the Savior. We as individuals and as a church must find concrete and meaningful avenues for our children to discover the joy of discipleship with Jesus.

Children need and want Jesus. We are told that children will finish the final proclamation of the gospel message. When we have properly discipled, baptized, and taught them, they are better grounded for genuine godly relationship and service, now and in the future.

Modeling

It was a pretty Sabbath morning and the church halls were filled with people entering the sanctuary. A tearful woman shyly approached me. Leaning in very close, she whispered, "My child was baptized years ago, but no one ever studied the doctrines with him or even told him about Jesus' plan of redemption. Did it take? Maybe I let him get baptized too young. Now he is seventeen, and he has never really understood our beliefs or expressed an interest in Jesus."

The problem was not his age; the problem was that we have forgotten the Master Teacher's design for making and keeping disciples. The stronger their bonds, the higher the likelihood they will remain in relationship with Christ.

Occasionally people substitute trick candles for the traditional candles on a birthday cake. When the birthday person blows out the trick candles, they relight in seconds, to the delight of the celebrants. When children connect to Jesus, their commitment is sincere and strong. Then life brings winds of confusion, gusts of pressure, and hurricanes of trial, and we think the flame of conversion has been blown out. But God has always been in the business of restoring dim and flickering lights. He provides the Holy Spirit to rekindle the flame of the light of Jesus. Our job is to seat the candle firmly in relationship to the Savior and King and to model living discipleship to those we bring to Jesus. Had that been the case for this seventeen-year-old, his mother may not have needed to ask the question.

The Bible records instances when large numbers of people were converted. But Heaven celebrates each person, whatever the age, who comes to Christ. The consistent, healthy new believers are those grounded not only in truth, but also in personal, discipling relationships; those who are provided opportunities and training for witnessing. Christ discipled His core group to disciple others, and then He commissioned them to service. More important than large numbers of converts are individual converts who are discipled and who provide lasting testimonies of a vibrant relationship with God and His people.

"Pastor," asked the dripping wet child, fresh out of the baptismal water, "what do I get to do now that I am 'missioned?" Have we thought about what we get to do now that we are commissioned? Perhaps intentional service should be part of what we cover when we prepare our children for baptism and membership.

Our children stay in Bible study class on at least two full rotations, not by design, but by choice. They, like adults, desire fellowship and need the reinforcement of other young believers. They love it when they get to "practice" and "teach" the lesson to the other students. One evening Derek came in and announced it was time for us to have prayer meeting for kids. During our parent-and-pastor time, we discovered that Derek has a leaning toward the gift of teaching and a melancholy/

sanguine temperament. Many evenings Derek leads the children to share their blessings and where God is moving in their lives. Children's attachment to Jesus is very real, and they need to be placed in meaningful service.

At a recent Children's Day, a six-year-old ministered to us by making the altar call. In his simple and direct way he shared his desire to be in heaven and his love for Jesus. As a result, more than a dozen children came forward to give their lives to Jesus, and several have begun baptismal studies. Our Adventurers come in full dress uniform to lift the offering, our morning prayer is offered by whole families, our children accompany parents and care providers to read the morning scripture, and children provide worship with music that is powerful and pure. Children's service to adults and other children demonstrates that all service is gifted and valued when done for Jesus.

The tremendous opportunities for development that come with ministry to and for children sometimes squeeze from us the expression "Help me to endure my blessings, Lord!" I have often wondered if the little children that Jesus blessed (see Mark 15) challenged the disciples as severely as the little ones challenge our time and resources today. We easily judge the disciples as being insensitive and uncaring, while perhaps overlooking the modern parallel.

The disciples obviously had close association with children in their own families and communities. They had observed other rabbis blessing children and must certainly have observed Jesus' tender regard for the little ones and others whom society undervalued. Despite the general warmth or personal connection to individual children, they did not grasp their inherent value. Similarly, many today find themselves "loving children," but remain disconnected from the reality that the Savior's salvation plan includes them.

A few months ago a fellow pastor called and asked how he could encourage his church to allocate some funding for children's ministries. It seems that the board had stated that they were already providing Sabbath School lesson papers and quarterlies, what more did they want? A few thoughts on the attitudes of the disciples might add insight and clarity to a dilemma such as this.

In responding to this question, it's important to remember that the Great Commission to all nations includes not only cultures, countries, and communities, but also groups and classes of people. It is a profound concept that Christ made an extraordinarily inclusive commission to reach all humanity. The same fervor and resources invested in adults must be exercised in claiming little souls whom He purchased with His blood—and perhaps even more, as children are "the claim of His love."[1]

As we see earth's chapters closing, the urgency of fulfilling our commission to reach our children should press heavy on our hearts. Maybe we have unintentionally missed something. Perhaps we have burned some bridges because of our attitudes and methods of communication in the past. The time has come to carefully reexamine the life of Jesus and seek methods and hearts that mirror His. Our commission comes with the empowering and equipping needed to fulfill it. Let's include the children as witnesses for the Master—committed, discipled, and commissioned. And let's *intentionally* target the lost children of this earth, that it may be said "of such is the kingdom of God."

1. Ellen G. White, *The Desire of Ages* (Nampa, Idaho: Pacific Press, 1941), 517.

To see the vision statement for children's ministry that Victoria Harrison's church has developed and the baptismal vows they use, go to www.adventistbookcenter.com/olink.tpl?sku=0816319987.

Become a Visionary for Children's and Youth Ministry

by Dexter Richardson

Dexter Richardson runs a coaching company and practices law in North Carolina. He and his wife, Jose, are licensed foster parents. Dexter has been involved in children's and youth ministries as a summer-camp director, high-school teacher, and pastor.

Because Adventist youth are leaving the church in large numbers, church members and leaders must come together and tackle the challenges creatively, pragmatically, and redemptively, using new ideas and methods. What would it take to make our church a place our children want to attend? I envision a church ministry to children and youth that provides dynamic and spiritual ministries, each one based upon biblical principles that teach how to honor God, respect others, and develop leadership skills that serve the local and worldwide church with a powerful Christian witness.

Before we look at strategies and ideas, however, let's celebrate the good things that we already have in place. First, there are the Sabbath School programs. Developing teams in the various divisions that provide imaginative, relevant, biblically based programming is the key to making these programs work. The Adventurer and Pathfinder Clubs have also had an amazing impact upon the young folks in our churches. These clubs provide opportunities for leadership, team building, and spiritual and intellectual growth. And the Adventist Youth programs on Sabbath afternoons not only teach and communicate religious themes, but also give our young people the opportunity to use their creativity, to develop public speaking and organizational skills, and to learn how to work effectively with people.

Summer-camp programs have touched the lives of our youth in a positive manner. And in recent years, our church has begun developing campus ministries that extend beyond Seventh-day Adventist campuses to reach Adventist and non-Adventist students attending public and private colleges and universities. These foundational programs give us something to build upon as we create and establish new ministries to meet the ongoing needs and concerns of our future leaders.

Suggested Strategies

1. Learn what's going on. In order to minister to our children and youth, we must know something about their world. Willingness to enter the world of other people shows our respect for them and gives us the opportunity to dialogue with them on a real level. Jesus did this very thing, which is one of the reasons His ministry was so effective.

To enter the world of our young people, we must engage them in personal conversations to get glimpses of things that matter to them. We may also gain information by studying the research that has been conducted about children and youth inside and outside of our church. Attending youth forums presented by various denominations and other organizations that work with young people also helps. Let's work on increasing our awareness level of the children and youth we seek to reach.

2. Acknowledge the presence of our young folks. Our children and youth should sense that they are as significant as any other members of our congregations. They must know that they are not less important because they are younger. We can begin to communicate this the moment they walk through the doors of the church. What would be wrong with taking a few minutes to interact with the children through an energetic hello, a warm handshake, or even some conversation? Prior to or during the worship service is also a good time to recognize birthdays, major accomplishments, and other key happenings in their lives.

One Sabbath I attended a local church where the minister took the time to recognize the young people who were going away to school. He prayed for them as a group and suggested that his members write and encourage them during the school year. This was a special moment as the students realized the love and support extended to them.

3. *Involve the children and youth in the planning and conducting of church life.* Church services and programs have a greater impact on members when they are directly involved in producing them. This means the planning committees must be made up of people representing the various constituents. Don't add just a token young person. Involving a number of young people will bring different points of view to the table. The various planning committees can provide new ideas for the church to ponder and execute new ministries serving every member of the congregation.

Perhaps the greatest immediate impact can be made by developing a worship committee. This committee should consist of people from all spectrums of the church congregation. It works in conjunction with the pastor to suggest ideas and ways to make the worship experience address the needs of the entire church. The planning and worship committees will permit our children and youth to gain a sense of ownership in their church and will bring new dimensions to the overall experience of the community of faith.

4. *Make sure the children and youth know that Jesus loves them.* A key ingredient in reaching our young people is teaching them about God's unconditional love and grace. Without this focus as our starting point, our ministries miss the mark. " 'God so loved the world that he gave his one and only Son, that whoever believes in him shall not perish but have eternal life. For God did not send his Son into the world to condemn the world, but to save the world through him' " (John 3:16, 17, NIV). This verse sounds so simple, but it is basic to effective ministry. If our young people could walk into our churches and find them to be centers of God's love and grace, this would significantly change the way they see the church. They should be able to see the unconditional love of God demonstrated through programming and through how we interact with them.

Getting Into the World of Children and Youth

Here's a list of ideas to stimulate your thinking about serving the children and youth in your church:

- Start a think tank that addresses the children's and youth ministries your church needs.
- Read books on children's and/or youth ministry.
- Take the opportunity to talk with at least one child at your church each Sabbath.
- Ask a child what he or she thinks would make the church program more exciting.
- Form a prayer group that focuses on the children and youth.
- Volunteer to help parents during the worship service who need assistance with their children.
- Take the time to learn more about the world of the children through playing with them.
- Implement a story hour or other children's program that runs concurrently with prayer meeting.
- Develop a puppet ministry at your church.
- Volunteer to do the children's story. Tell stories that are short and to the point and that teach moral and spiritual lessons.
- Organize regular game and video nights at your church.
- Get involved with activities such as Pathfinders, Sabbath School, Vacation Bible School, summer camps, and Adventist Youth meetings.
- Visit children's functions—children's museums, bookstores, toy stores, etc.—to observe what avenues are used to reach children.
- Encourage young people to get involved in Habitat for Humanity, art shows, feeding the homeless, helping older people, and similar endeavors.
- Get your children involved in one of the local missions for Thanksgiving or Christmas dinner or help them make food baskets to give to the needy in your community.
- Adopt a child or become a foster parent.

- Volunteer to baby sit to experience children up close and give the parents an evening off.
- Get involved in or start a campus ministries program at the local college or university in your community.
- Serve as a mentor to a child or youth.
- Help organize a church sports league (baseball, soccer, basketball, etc.).
- Plan a mission trip with the help of your local conference.
- Invite children and youth to participate regularly in the worship services through music, drama, Scripture reading, storytelling, and other avenues.
- Implement children's and youth music ministries.
- Take photos and videos of the youth events in your church, and present these as a program to the church at large.
- Sponsor a youth.

CHAPTER 14

Church for Children

by Jean Sequeira

Jean Sequeira is a freelance writer and seminar speaker who enjoyed working as a pastor's wife, Bible instructor, missionary teacher, and as an editorial secretary for the Adventist Review. She now writes from Keizer, Oregon.

When I was seventeen and living in North London, England, God touched my life and I joyfully surrendered my heart to Him. He took that life, turned it around, and set my feet on unexpected paths. From that time on I had a Father who loved and provided for me and whose promises were true, and a church full of loving people who took me into their hearts.

One unforgettable day some dear soul took me by the hand and led me to the little back room where children of all ages, from birth to juniors, met together for Sabbath School. She informed me that I had just been appointed their leader—quite a daunting prospect for someone who had never attended a children's Sabbath School class! I didn't think of refusing this challenge, and somehow, through a lot of prayer and learning experiences, the children and I managed to get through those years until I went away to Newbold College. The fact that today one of those children is a union communication director bears no reflection on my talents, but rather serves to show how God can take even the most unlikely willing vessel and put it to use. Sometimes God surprises us.

He certainly surprised me many years later when, as a grandmother, I naively volunteered to care for my three grandchildren, then eight, four, and two, while my son Christopher and his wife, Nenette, took a well-needed vacation to celebrate their tenth wedding anniversary. I say naive only because this was something new for me since my husband and I had only recently retired and moved three thousand miles across country to be near them.

I can still see the odd socks and the inside-out sweater that met my tired gaze Sabbath morning as we piled out of the car and headed toward the church. I had the distinct feeling that from that moment on, every time I went to church and saw a family coming through the doors, I would let out a cheer that they had actually made it at all. And I would definitely be more compassionate toward moms and dads of any age who sit in church trying to handle their squirming children.

Do we as church members make our children and youth feel welcome when they come to church? I recall an old adage passed around our churches some years ago: "Crying babies are like good committee actions—they should be carried out!" Instead of carrying them out, we, as the family of God, should be willing to do all that we can to keep them in the church. One way of doing this is by having a special service on Sabbath mornings just for the children. Some call it Children's Church.

Children's Church

What is Children's Church? It is a service that

- is specifically designed to meet the needs of our children;
- reaches children's hearts and prepares them to make a decision for Christ;
- helps children build a relationship with Jesus;
- explains the Scriptures in easy-to-understand language;
- helps children understand the practicality of God's Word;
- teaches children to memorize texts for recall later as needed;
- helps children to apply biblical principles to their lives;
- familiarizes children with the doctrines of the church;
- provides fellowship with other children;
- teaches stories that contain lessons on moral development;
- trains children to willingly share the good news with others.

While there will always be members who feel that the place of the children is in the pew with their parents, there are many others who realize that what works best for adults is not always the best for the children. Remember that children are not little adults, and their needs should be taken into consideration.

Next time you are in church, take time to observe the children around you. Why do they need to be occupied with the contents of their Sabbath bags? It's because their attention span is very short, and while we adults might be totally engrossed with the brilliant sermon being presented, that same forty-five minutes seems like a long time to a child. Add to that the fact that a little child probably cannot even see where the voice is coming from, and the problem becomes obvious. It has always perplexed me that we expect children to have a Sabbath School program full of child-oriented music, child-sized furniture, and children's activities and then expect them to settle down for an hour in an adult environment where, very often, their feet don't even reach to the floor. That's not the most comfortable position for anyone. So why not provide an occasional meeting geared especially to the children that prepares them for the adult worship service?

How can we make church more meaningful to children? By considering their needs instead of our own. You'll find an excellent overview of Children's Church on the North American Division Web site <www.childmin.com>.

How Others Do It

Paris, France: The largest Seventh-day Adventist Church in Paris has seven hundred members on its books, but nine hundred people attend each week. Pastor Hebert Valiame told me that in order to make room for all the adults in the main sanctuary, youthful and enthusiastic volunteers hold a Children's Church three Sabbaths a month. On the fourth Sabbath the children attend the adult church service.

Capital Memorial Church, Washington, D.C.: When effervescent Gini Taylor was asked to be the children's ministries leader at her church in Washington, D.C., her great love for children moved her to take up the challenge. She planned her Children's Church, which meets once a month—she believes children should also learn to sit in church with their parents—to teach the children about God and the plan of salvation and about Jesus and ways to serve Him according to the stages of their development.

The program she developed caters to three- to twelve-year-olds. The venue is a senior-division Sabbath School room rather than a children's Sabbath School room. This prevents the little congregation from becoming distracted by materials left in the room and on the walls from previous children's classes. It also means that set-up can be done ahead of time.

Gini prepared her own gospel-centered programs containing stories using puppets handled by the teens or visitors, Bible-oriented crafts, picture coloring, cutouts, topical items, skits, and Bible themes. When videos are shown, the children are given a list of questions to be answered at the end of the program. This helps to keep their minds focused on the topic. The program is based on the format of the regular church worship service, with children doing Scripture readings, special music, and whatever else they're willing to do. The Children's Church program receives $500 annually from the church to cover the cost of supplies and incidentals.

Gini has now handed the responsibility of this program on to others. Teams of helpers are made up of four people—many of whom first learned to work with children by participating in these programs. Others are Sabbath School teachers who know the children and have a love of service in their hearts. They are happy whenever teens or younger children want to participate because they understand that children learn through doing. Many parents accompany their little ones for Children's Church, and this is encouraged since the parents help with crowd control and any difficult children.

One outstanding program was a reenactment of the Last Supper, with the helpers dressed in biblical costumes. They first acted out the Supper, explaining the symbols of bread and wine and the Passover lamb. Then they mingled with the children around the tables set up in the shape of a cross. The children were given whole-wheat flat bread to eat and a glass of grape juice to drink, and they enjoyed fruit from beautifully arranged baskets—a typical Mediterranean meal.

Gini feels it is important to remember that Children's Church is not a repetition of Sabbath School. She notes that since this is a multi-age group, it can be more challenging. And she counsels that Children's Church leaders should make sure children use the restroom facilities before entering the room—it makes for fewer interruptions by the children during program time.

The children at Capitol Memorial Church know they are loved; they look forward to being with the teams who introduce them to the Christ who's the center of Christianity.

East Salem Seventh-day Adventist Church: All the way across the other side of the United States lives Gary Parks, senior pastor of the East Salem Seventh-day Adventist Church in Salem, Oregon. He has a unique outlook when it comes to Children's Church. He believes that church services should be planned for children so that children know what church is for and what it's all about. His philosophy is that we should allow children to be part of the church service.

Having three children of his own must help to form his thinking, because Pastor Gary has many innovative, child-related ideas. He holds Children's Church in the main sanctuary with the adults four times a year and advertises the dates well in advance so families can mark their calendars and be sure not to miss those worship services. When those Sabbaths arrive, families and children sit up near the front of the sanctuary.

Children participate in the service by serving as deacons, reading Scripture, performing special music, taking up the collection, offering prayer, singing in praise teams, and participating in skits. They even present the story time (for adults!). Pastor Gary believes that every child has a gift, and his dream is to have his elders ensure that everyone at church has a job to fulfill.

Because his program takes place during the regular worship time, the teams of helpers usually required for Children's Church are not necessary. Instead, Pastor Gary relies on the church's worship committee, which is already in place. Using this kind of program also means that there's no need for a special budget—a blessing to churches whose budgets are already tight.

During the sermon time, Pastor Gary presents Christ-centered illustrations geared to helping the children see how God can work in their lives. He explains the good news of the gospel in simple language so they can understand and are prepared to entrust their hearts and lives to Jesus.

How do the members of the congregation react to this unusual approach? Many have said that because of Children's Church they have a better understanding of the gospel since it is presented in simpler terms on those occasions. Church members say they avoid planning weekends in the mountains or along the coast on the Children's Church Sabbaths because neither they nor their children want to miss them. When East Salem has Children's Church, the whole congregation is blessed.

Doctor Richard M. Davidson, a seminary professor at Andrews University in Berrien Springs, Michigan, shares an experience that happened when he was a young pastor working in Arizona. The youngest members of his congregation were in their sixties. While he was preaching one Sabbath, a visitor's baby started crying. The sound reverberated through the sanctuary, making the young pastor wonder to whom the congregation would be listening—the baby or him. His thoughts took a 180-degree turn when the aged elder who prayed the closing prayer said, "And thank You, Lord, for the sound of a baby crying once again in this church."

Are you appreciative of the children in your church? Do they see Jesus in you?

CHAPTER 15

Surviving and Thriving in a Multi-age Sabbath School

by Aileen Andres Sox

Aileen Andres Sox, editor of Our Little® Friend *and* Primary Treasure® *at Pacific Press® Publishing Association, Nampa, Idaho, spent twenty years of her adult life in Primary Sabbath Schools and likes to share with others the methods she has found make them run more smoothly.*

You run a little Sabbath School in a little church. Six kids come faithfully each week, and three others show up occasionally. They vary in age from three to twelve. However on earth can you have a meaningful Sabbath School in such circumstances?

Reframe how you see Sabbath School. I suggest you think of your Sabbath School in terms of family worship. In family worship you might have age spans from parents to teens to toddlers. The atmosphere should be happy and relaxed. When I was a teenager in my "blended family" home, we found that stories kept everyone's attention pretty well. In recent years I have learned that activities are another way to keep everyone's attention. The *GraceLink* materials describe many different activities that you can choose from.[1]

Get the kids to help. In a family, older kids help younger ones. In my home I was nine years older than my sister and thirteen years older than my youngest brother. I loved making sure that they got the help they needed when we did things together as a family. Around my church now I see many kids, girls especially, who excel in watching and entertaining our toddlers. Take advantage of this! Assign the older kids in your Sabbath School the task of teaching a finger play or song to the toddler. Do them together each week, adding new ones as appropriate. (The Beginner *GraceLink* materials have plenty to suggest.) Older children will enjoy singing favorite "little kid" songs too. And look at the daily activities for Beginners and Kindergartners for age-appropriate things to do with the younger kids. Spend perhaps one-third of your Sabbath School time on the younger ones.

You may need to meet with your older children at some special time, like breakfast in a restaurant or over vegeburgers at your house, to explain that you need their help to have a Sabbath School that is enjoyable for everyone. Ask them what would make it seem like a happy family time. Use their suggestions. You'll have to remind them from time to time that you need their cooperation. With positive reinforcement, they'll do very well most of the time.

Get another adult to help. When you have a lot of ages in one room, you will need another adult to help too. I just read about a Sabbath School where, after enjoying activities together, the three-year-old is happy to color for a while during the older children's lesson. That toddler's mother is there to help supervise her child, but at the same time, as a new Christian, she is drinking in all that the older kids are learning. Perhaps the other adult could tell the mission story each week. Be sure to try the games and foods from the country the story comes from. Kids of all ages love that!

Pick which lesson you'll study in Sabbath School, but provide age-appropriate materials for home. In most cases the Primary *GraceLink* materials will work best for your multi-age room. Do those activities and study that lesson (along with the special things for your toddler discussed above). Look at the suggestions for daily worship for other activities that might work better for your small group. Children should also get their own age-appropriate lesson to study at home. Consider having a Friday evening or Sabbath afternoon program for Juniors and Earliteens, when they can study their own lesson.

Take it to God. I'm continually dumbfounded at how God changes circumstances when we ask. Our church hadn't held a Vacation Bible School for a number of years. We had no idea how Bug Safari would turn out. At our training session, we promised to pray each day at 4:00 P.M. for VBS. We asked, among other things, for enough volunteers and for children to come. We ended the week with fifty-five volunteers and a hundred children attending. Even more amazing, every volunteer was ready to "do it again next year."

Our leader's adult daughter Michelle ran VBS at her church in Colorado—another church that hadn't done VBS for a number of years. Prayer warriors met weekly to ask God to bless each child who would attend. Michelle reminded the church each Sabbath to pray also. Their goal was 150 children attending. They started the week with seventy and had 121 on the night with the most kids, with 149 different kids in all. They invited parents to a special VBS program on Sabbath morning. The church was packed at 9:30 A.M. One woman commented, "I have never seen anything like this in my entire life!"

Do you want more children each Sabbath? Talk about your dream with your church, especially the parents of the children you have now. Make a pact to pray about it. Encourage children to invite their friends. You should begin a separate class whenever you have three children of any age group.

Then watch and see what God does. Remember that He wants to partner with you for your sake as well as for the sake of others. He wants your church not just to survive but also to thrive—not because He loves big numbers but because He loves all people and wants them to know and love Him.

---

1. For excellent advice on combining ages, go to <www.gracelink.com> and the Sabbath School organization section of Frequently Asked Questions. At <http://www.maucsda.org>, which is the Web site for the Mid-America Union Conference, you'll find the Center for Small Church Revitalization. The Mid-America Union Conference *Outlook* magazine contains dozens of good ideas to promote church growth. And *Sunday School Specials* from Group Publishing discusses multi-aged classes that include parents. Each of the *Specials* provides thirteen multi-aged programs. You will want to stick with the *GraceLink* materials, but it is good to know how other people make multi-age classes work.

See That No One Misses Grace

by Noelene Johnsson

Noelene Johnsson, director of the Children's Ministries Department of the North American Division, notes that while children today live with incredible pain, pressure, and enticements, churches have a wonderful opportunity to provide families a haven of healing and grace.

Many years ago Maureen Luxton, an associate director of the General Conference Sabbath School department, observed: "No matter what you do, God never stops loving you. This is the single most important message we can teach Adventist children and youth." She wanted to plant this message firmly in the minds of Adventist young people because it would serve them well if they ever strayed. People who remember the grace of God can more easily find their way back because they don't have to worry about how God will treat them.

The creators of *GraceLink* lessons for children take seriously the admonition of Hebrews 12:15, "See to it that no one misses the grace of God" (NIV), because they realize that it is by grace that our children are saved (Eph. 2:5). God demonstrated grace most fully at Calvary. When Jesus said, "I, when I am lifted up from the earth, will draw all [persons] to myself" (John 12:32, NIV), He was stating a fact: Grace draws us to Jesus. And Jesus is the best protection from temptation.

GraceLink, the church's twenty-first century curriculum for children's Sabbath School, is carefully designed not only to teach children about the gospel and salvation but also to help them value and respond to grace.

GraceLink *emphasizes grace one month of every four.* Grace is the vertical relationship: God loving me, favoring me, though I don't deserve it.

Grace is Jesus carrying the cross for me and willingly dying the death that I deserve so that I could enjoy the forever life that He deserves. There's nothing I can do to make God love me more; nothing I can do to make Him love me less. What a God!

GraceLink *focuses on worship one month of every four.* Worship is my response to God's grace. Ellen White, speaking of the "unsearchable riches of His grace," states, "As you contemplate these riches, you will come into possession of them."[1] In other words, making grace a focal point of worship makes it real in our lives—and in our lifestyle.

When I contemplate grace, my heart overflows in praise, prayer, songs, and devotion. Grace motivates submission and obedience to God's law. Notice that grace and obedience have a cause/effect relationship; they are not opposite as some would have us believe. Legalism, obeying for the wrong reasons, is the opposite of grace. It is God's "power to present you without spot and blameless."[2] Our own effort can't accomplish that. *GraceLink* lessons emphasize worship to the same extent that they do grace.

Community *is a third dynamic of* **GraceLink** *and is also studied one month of every four.* Children learn that community is the horizontal, "I love you" relationship between themselves and others in God's family. Like worship, community is a response to God's grace. Community means that I value others and accept them just as they are—not because of what they have or have done, but for themselves—just as Jesus accepts me.

In the family of God I am loved and accepted and I learn to love and accept others without respect to any factor that would otherwise tend to divide us, be it age, gender, culture, language, skin color, physical disability, or style of dress. And in the family of God, each one is needed and valued. If the entire church would pay more attention to community, what wonderfully safe havens our churches would be for kids!

Service *is the fourth and final* **GraceLink** *dynamic.* Service is my relationship with others who are not part of our church community. Service says, "I love you too." It is my recognition of God's favor toward those who do not know Him as I do. My service witnesses to my love for God, earning me the right to talk about Him with those I serve.

Helping Kids Catch On to Grace

GraceLink lessons for children are printed in warm, friendly colors so children know that their church really cares about them. But children do not experience grace through printed materials alone; the materials draw their attention to the grace that already exists in their lives. Grace is caught rather than taught—caught from interaction with grace-filled parents and teachers, caught from instances of unconditional love.

Grace is *caught* when parents and teachers:

- Give every child the same reward, those who need lots of prompting as well as those with a perfect record or perfect recall.
- Give the occasional treat for no special reason other than that they want to.
- Refuse to let any child become invisible or marginalized.
- Value every child to the same degree.
- Accept all responses in a discussion, finding ways to draw value from each.
- Seek out the shy or rebellious children and befriend them.
- Let kids live with the consequences of their actions, not rubbing it in but showing extra kindness and concern.
- Trust children while at the same time recognizing that any child will misbehave if not kept busy and involved.
- Refuse to post attendance charts on the wall lest they embarrass those children who would like to attend faithfully but cannot through no fault of their own.
- Refuse to distinguish between children on the basis of physical characteristics, be it eye color, hair color, height, weight, or intelligence.

Grace is *taught* when children:

- Participate in carefully designed activities, provided the activity is followed by meaningful questions that elicit thoughtful discussion.
- Are introduced to the lesson at church and urged to study more during the week, not in order to show their knowledge the following week, but out of love for God and for His Word.

- Study every day with a parent or by phone with a teacher or classmate.
- Phone someone else to help them learn the lesson or text.
- Form prayer trios: Three persons meet together; each states what God is telling them from the lesson texts and is prayed for by the other two. They pray right there together and then separately during the coming week. The trio meets again in a week to hold each other accountable for following through on what God asked them to do. They then repeat the process for the new lesson.
- Learn to look for grace in any given Bible story.
- Are constantly reminded that worship, community, and service are their response to grace.
- Are reminded that they are saved by grace alone; good works are their way of telling God thank You and of staying in His grace.
- Hear grace stories.

GraceLink has a feature designed to ensure that the lessons stick: the weekly lesson theme—a brief message that summarizes the main point of the lesson. The activities and discussion opportunities throughout a *GraceLink* Sabbath School keep bringing the students back to the message of the lesson so that by the time they leave, they have memorized the message. The key Bible text is also referred to along with the message. Children not only leave knowing what they learned, but they make this message part of their lives. When God is prompting a strayed child of His to return, we want that child to remember these key messages of grace that can make the way home all the more appealing.

It Takes a Church

According to an old African proverb, it takes a village to raise a child. Similarly, it takes an entire church to protect and save the children.

It takes a pastor who continually reminds the church that childhood, ages five through thirteen, is the window of opportunity for accepting Jesus.[3]

It takes a church finance committee that plans a budget that recognizes the priority of ministry to children and sees the cost as an investment, not an expenditure.

It takes a nominating committee willing to prioritize children's and youth leadership appointments, making selections based on the nominees' love for children and youth, spiritual gifts, and skills in communicating with the age level. After all, if children are our future, should we not assure that future by assigning our most dedicated and gifted to teach them?

It takes church elders who care enough to make the effort to observe what is happening in children's programs and pastors interested enough to ask what is being taught in Sabbath School at every age level and to hold parents and teachers accountable for the spiritual growth of children.

It takes a Family Ministries Committee that plans parenting seminars on the spiritual nurture of children. Like Samson's parents in ancient times, today's Christian parents want to know how to raise their children in the fear of the Lord.

It takes a church social committee that plans occasions when the saints can have fun as a church, when youth can socialize in a safe environment, when the generations can learn to enjoy each other, when families can get to know other families. If children are included in the games, they learn to associate their church with good times and warm feelings.

It takes a Sabbath School leadership that arranges adult Sabbath School classes so that the parents of Kindergarten-age children, for instance, are assigned to the same class. That way the class dismisses ten minutes before the Kindergarten division does so that the parents can get down to their kids' class and surround the kids for the closing prayer. Not only do the kids look forward to this opportunity to demonstrate something that they learned or show something they made, but they get a sense that the parents—all the parents—care about them. (Imagine how important Juniors would feel if their parents did the same thing. But parents need to do this with confidence, knowing that they belong there and that their kids will remember this all their lives.)

It takes the commitment of every member to make church a friendly place for children and their families. All members need to be learning the names of the children and greeting them by name. All the members can be committees of one to tell kids they are glad they came. Research shows that the young adults who stay with the church are those who feel that their church knows them and cares. We will lose many of today's children—those sitting up front in church for the children's story—unless the adults of the church get to know their names and make them feel part of the community.

It also takes a church that is serious about protecting children by screening the volunteers who work with them and any other high-profile volunteers in the church whom children and youth may approach for mentoring. (Information about volunteer screening is available at <www.childmin.com>.) Longtime leaders and teachers may feel insulted when asked to fill out a ministry application form for screening purposes, but those who understand the pain and spiritual loss caused by sexual abuse agree that the effort is worth it to protect children and youth.

To keep our children safe, we must, above all, have a praying church. Everyone at church needs to pray for children and youth in general and several in particular by name. Members can ask God to surround the children with His Spirit of grace, bringing peace, protection, and joy. This Spirit is real, and His benefits are real too. Prayer makes a huge difference in the life of the one praying and the one being prayed for.

I am reminded again of the story of the party searching for a little child lost in the vast cornfields of the Midwest during a blizzard. When the searchers were ready to give up, the parents begged everyone to join hands and sweep the field one more time. They found the child, but it was too late. If only they had joined hands sooner!

In these last days when the public media is targeting children, it is time for the community of faith, the family of God, to join hands. We are in a war, and children and teens are the casualties. The church needs to mobilize; together we can counter the enemy attack. Let's join hands, take hold of God's grace, and, utilizing the power of prayer, neither give up nor admit defeat in the battle for the mind of the child living with us, the children worshiping with us, or of the child living next door.

---

1. Ellen G. White, *Acts of the Apostles* (Nampa, Idaho: Pacific Press, 1911), 567.

2. Ibid.

3. According to the Barna Research Group, as noted in a November 1999 news release (see <www.barna.org>).

Nine Reasons to Mentor Kids

by Jackie Bishop

Jackie Bishop is director of children's ministries in the Rocky Mountain Conference, a REAL learning specialist, and a co-writer for GraceLink. *This chapter is adapted from a seminar given at the 2002 Mid-America Union Ministries Convention in Kansas City, Kansas.*

Youth need mentors. Research shows that youth who are mentored are 46-70 percent less likely to do drugs, 27 percent less likely to initiate alcohol use, 53 percent less likely to skip class, 30 percent less likely to hit somebody, and more confident in their school work. A study in California showed that when kids had mentors other than family members, 98 percent of them stayed in school, 85 percent did not do drugs, and 97 percent didn't become teen parents. Mentoring almost always displaces the gang mentality—"hang out, skip school, be uninterested." Give kids a place to plug in and belong, and they don't desire that stuff.

There are adults who can influence kids' lives in ways that family members can't. I think every parent ought to be praying for that person whom God provides as a mentor. Chester's* father is an addict. His mother prayed for a father figure for Chester. Now a youth pastor in his early thirties has taken an interest in him. This pastor is talking to him about hard issues like pornography and masturbation, and Chester feels that he can open up with this guy.

This pastor has an interest in music. He goes into a recording studio and has Chester playing bass for him. This is what Chester really wanted

---

* "Chester" is a pseudonym.

to do—get involved in some sort of a musical band; now he works with the pastor on producing these little projects for his church and community. Chester's mother couldn't have provided this opportunity for him.

Here are nine reasons to mentor kids:

1. It instills values in our youth. You'd be amazed at how many children grow up in a home in which parents don't have a clue about what values they want to teach their children, much less have an idea about how to do it. Mentoring can help kids learn values that their family system can't give them.

2. It develops their leadership skills. Too many kids have come from critical, negative, "you can't do anything" parents who are afraid of what they're doing. All they hear is "You shouldn't be smoking, you shouldn't be staying out, your grades are bad, you shouldn't be this, you shouldn't be that." Even though parents have the best of intentions, they end up being so negative that the kids are just beaten down all the time. Someone outside the family can offer encouragement: "Wow, you really shine here! Your gifts are just amazing. Come on, I can help you grow in this area."

3. It improves self-confidence. The pastor looks at Chester like he's a big guy, so Chester feels like a big guy when he's around the pastor. Mentors can ignore all the family dynamics and treasure something about their "mentees" that maybe Mom hasn't seen or Dad can't quite get a handle on because he sees all the negatives.

4. It provides opportunities for counseling on life issues. Chester will tell his pastor stuff that he doesn't feel as comfortable talking to his mother about even though they seem to have a pretty open relationship. There's stuff that young people need other people for, people who aren't going to be critical or who have a different perspective on them.

5. It provides a model of serving others. Again, we're talking about just modeling here. When kids know that you care about them and see things happening in your life that are productive and positive and that's something that they want, they are much more likely to get involved in those kinds of things as well. Too often parents set up expectations, and then the kids want to rebel against them. "Mom said it was black, so I'll say it was white." Chester's going around now and telling his story because he sees the pastor doing that and he sees it working out for him. Chester's mother has been doing this for years, but Chester didn't decide to do it because his mom does it. A mentor has been the answer.

6. It decreases self-centeredness. Kids begin to look outside themselves when they've got somebody else paying attention to them. They don't need to work to get that attention anymore. They can begin to look out and share their giftedness with those ones around them.

7. It opens their minds to bigger possibilities. They see in the life of their mentor that there is something more out there than just trying to get through every day or trying to get over the latest punishment or the latest problem with Mom or Dad.

8. It makes them accountable. When mentors provide the right atmosphere, their mentees will begin to allow them and even invite them to hold them accountable. Chester's mother says that Chester and his pastor have a weekly conversation, which she says involves accountability for his pornography addiction. Chester told his mother, "Jim's going to be checking in with me, and I think it really helps to be able to say what I did and what I didn't do. Even if I messed up and did it, Jim doesn't yell at me or frown at me." So there's accountability, both personally and spiritually.

9. It develops resilience. A research project appearing in *U.S. News & World Report* found that one-third of the kids who grew up in chronically dysfunctional families turned out well. These are kids who come from really painful backgrounds: homes marred by drug addiction, alcoholism, sexual abuse, live-in boyfriends—really majorly dysfunctional. The researcher asked, "How come one-third of these kids seem to survive so well?" She found that it was outside influences that made the difference in the lives of these kids—people stepping in even though they didn't spend a whole lot of time in comparison to what the family time was. This suggests that an attentive adult could turn a mean and sullen kid, a kid who would smash into someone's face on a whim, into an upstanding Boy Scout. Just modeling and love.

Imagine what mentoring could do for some of the kids in your church! I think it is the power of grace.

Ministry to Youth

Filling the Vacuum

by Baraka G. Muganda

Baraka Muganda is the youth director of the General Conference of Seventh-day Adventists. He enjoys challenging youth to love and serve God. He believes that involving the youth is the secret to strengthening them spiritually and capturing their commitment to the mission of the church.

In Seventh-day Adventist homes, parents often take time to discuss what they would like to see happening in the secular lives of their children and the hobbies that are important to their children. They even discuss what vocations they want to see their young people take up. And they encourage their young people to study hard to become good citizens. Even more important, however, is the time taken to discuss spiritual concepts. Parents need to follow the counsel of Jesus: "Seek ye first the kingdom of God and His righteousness." If this is not uppermost in the lives of the parents as evidenced by their daily conduct and their church activities, the children will lack the example they need.

It's easy to blame the church when young people say they do not want to attend church. Some parents complain, "My child is no longer interested in church affairs because the church has poor programs. The church does not meet the expectations of our young people." They may repeat a long list of problems, forgetting that one of the main reasons their young people are not interested in church is that they have seen that their parents are not committed to Christ or the church. As a result the parents find themselves unable to give positive encouragement when their kids begin to fall away from Christ.

Many families carefully set aside and guard time for watching television and listening to radio programs that satisfy temporal desires. But they preserve no special time for reading the Sabbath School lesson or even for praising the Lord with a few songs. They give only their "leftover" time—time that is not so important.

Josh Billings rephrased Proverbs 22:6 as follows: "Train up a child in the way he should go—and walk there yourself once in a while." He meant that if you want your child to love the church, then you need to be in the habit of walking the talk—going to church on a regular basis, for example. Billings was saying that you cannot train up children without you, as a parent, being involved. You must convince your children that you also enjoy walking in the way they should go, and you do this through your daily behavior.

We teach by example—by reading the Bible, by singing of Jesus' soon coming and about the Friend we have in Jesus. When Dad and Mom sing spiritual songs in their home, their children will grow up with these songs in their hearts.

What do our kids see in us? Do they see parents who care more for their spiritual destiny than their temporal success? Some parents say that their children cannot go to a campout or other fellowship event because they don't make friends easily or they have some other problem. The children grow up without a yearning for youth camp or other youth fellowship programs because the parents have programmed them in a negative path.

A Pathfinder Club invited their members to display their favorite hobbies. A young person who was not a Pathfinder called and wanted to exhibit his coin collection. The director pointed out that he was not a member and encouraged him to join the club. Later it was learned that this young boy's parents would have let him join—if he paid the dues out of his allowance. The message these parents sent to this child was that they didn't really care if he belonged. This young man is now married and has children of his own, but he no longer belongs to our church. Of course, a lot of other factors may have influenced him negatively, but parental encouragement and interest in a child's activities remains absolutely essential.

Parents, care for the destiny of your young people. Guiding them in the path we want them to travel remains the most important parental responsibility. And leading the way, walking on that path ourselves, is an essential part of providing that guidance.

Billy Graham says, "Parents have little time for children and a great vacuum has developed and into that vacuum is going to move some kind of ideology." Parents need to fill this vacuum with something valuable. If the church and the parents are not careful, satanic ideologies, atheism, New Age thinking, cartoons, rock and roll, and a myriad of other time-consuming distractions may fill this vacuum. If you want your child to be a Christian and to enjoy eternal life, you must fill the vacuum with spiritual things, so when your children grow up, they will say, "I want Christ in my life. I want to follow the truth."

It has been said, "Give me a child the first six years of his life and you can do what you will with him thereafter." In my country, Tanzania, we have many Muslims in our cities, and at every junction there is a mosque. During the week, little Muslim children between one and six years old are brought to be taught about the "Great Prophet Mohammed" every day. It is almost impossible to convert Muslims, because from early childhood all they know is the Koran. They know Prophet Mohammed and not Prophet Jesus.

Does eternal destiny matter? Yes. So, parents, let's reorganize our priorities and fill the vacuum all children have with spiritual activities and influences to prepare them to live for Jesus every day of their lives.

CHAPTER 19

God Works in the Lives of the Young

by James Black

James Black is director of youth and Pathfinder ministries in the North American Division. He says he's dedicated his life to helping young people realize their potential for God's kingdom. The chapter that follows is based on Myrna Tetz's interview of him.

Just before my high-school graduation one of my atheist teachers decided to fail me because of a technicality on a final report. I told him that my God was going to change this situation. He responded, "You can pray to God all you want, but He can't control me." When I told my mother about this she said, "You know, son, this is going to be your first testing battle. It's time for you to see what God is going to do personally in your life." To make a long story short, I saw God change a situation that I thought was impossible. That gave me the foundation for a belief that God is real even for young people. Subsequently, I went on to Oakwood College and accepted the call to ministry.

When I became a minister, my burden was to show young people that the same God who fought my battle could fight theirs. I continue to tell my story of losing my brother in gang violence at age seventeen and almost losing my own life at age thirteen. I don't want young people to go through what we went through. My life's mission is to give something or share something that will help some young person avoid the pitfalls that I experienced. So, my personal experience led me to youth ministry. My whole approach to youth ministry is that things can be better if you have some direction, and my life is now dedicated to helping youth find that direction, to helping them to see Jesus.

But even when you're ministering for God, things don't always work the way you wish they would. My wife and I had been working with a young single girl, a member of the church, who had decided to have an abortion. We spent a lot of time trying to be spiritual mentors, but it seemed like our efforts were fruitless. We thought we were making progress, but she had made her decision. "I've got four kids," she said. "I can't have another, and I now realize that the guy who got me pregnant does not love me. I've got to do this."

We did the best we could to try to show her that there are better options—even if you carry the child full term and give it up for adoption. But she got an abortion. This floors you as a leader, because you've prayed, you've done your best, you've done all the things that you thought were right, and still this happens. Regardless of the outcome, we still have to give this girl hope. Spiritually, mentally, and emotionally she continues to struggle. The next time we saw her we just put our arms around her, cried with her, and assured her that we are going to love her just as God loves her. Some might think that a condemning sermon would have been appropriate; we didn't think so. Most importantly, we wanted her to know that the same God who picks us up will pick her up. This has been a growing experience—not getting immediate, positive results, while still having to remain shepherds for the sheep.

There are a few other situations that I want to share about troubled youth—a couple points I'd like to make that I think are crucial. Sometimes we pigeonhole youth in the church as "troubled" or "untroubled" based on rumors or obvious outward signs—for example, having children outside of marriage or smelling like smoke or alcohol or having a reputation for partying and playing the girls/guys. But what about the youth who don't look like they are troubled? I would venture to say that a significant number of them are seriously troubled, but because they don't look the part, we don't know how to minister to them. We are better at ministering in crisis situations than at ministering to everyone because it's the right thing to do.

Ministering to the "Untroubled"

It's troubling to think that we miss ministering to so many youth because their trouble is not obvious. The last two young persons I buried committed suicide. Interestingly, neither one of them looked troubled. No one knew they were troubled. No one knew they had issues. Of course, the church wanted to know, "What can we do now? How can we prevent this from happening again? How do we put our arms around our young people?" It was amazing to see how the churches rallied around the young people because of a crisis. But then, news is only interesting while it's interesting. When the crises pass, it's back to business as usual until it happens again. I'm really concerned about the unidentified troubled youth who have issues that are not obvious. We must minister to these kids. Jesus would.

One more situation to give balance to my concerns: When I was the youth director for the Southwest Region Conference, I got a call from my mom. "Did you know that Maurice [my nephew] is in jail? I'm not sure what it is for." We went home the following weekend and got him out of jail. He was in jail for a carjacking incident. He claims he got in the car with some friends and didn't know the car was stolen. I'm thinking, *The sun is shining where it's snowing, and I forgot which planet I'm on.* Before I got him out of jail, I said to him, "Maurice, if you're not careful, you won't live to be twenty-one years old." At the time he was seventeen—the same age as my brother who died in gang violence.

I got him out of jail and came back to Dallas. About a month later he called. "Uncle James," he said. "I need to come live with you. If I don't come to Dallas, I'm going to die in Georgia." My wife and I agreed, and he came out immediately. The following month we had a Thanksgiving youth retreat—young people came for five days of spiritual renewal during the Thanksgiving holidays. As we were closing one of the sessions, I noticed Maurice was not there, and I'm thinking, *Oh man, Maurice should have been here. God could have touched him if he'd heard this great presentation.* I thought Maurice was on the lake fishing or something.

I'm standing up front, getting ready to give the closing prayer, and Maurice runs into the building and toward the platform. I'm seeing this young man who is 6' 2," you know, tears running down his face. He grabs the microphone from me, and I'm thinking, *He's lost his mind.* But Maurice turns to the two hundred kids in the building and says, "I want all of you to know that God is real." And I'm standing there with my mouth open. I'm stunned. Everyone is stunned. He proceeds to share with the young people that while he didn't even want to come to the meeting, God spoke to him and said, "Maurice, if you just give Me a chance, I'll blow your mind." And he said, "OK, God, take it." Maurice told the group, "I know now that God is real, and I've got Him." And that turned the whole retreat around—kids were crying and giving their hearts to God.

Some people thought it was a temporary fix, but they were wrong. Since then Maurice graduated from Southwestern Adventist University with degrees in business and religion. Currently he is working as a healthcare administrator. It's one of those stories that involve a rough situation, but the enemy didn't get the outcome he wanted. Maurice has told his story all around the country. He is preaching up a storm all over the place and doing a great job for God. So this gives a balance to the suicide and abortion situations. There are many other stories about young people out there that have positive endings as well.

I think that one of the main things we need in the church right now is patience. The problem is that we take a microwave approach in dealing with our young people: We want them done now. We want immediate results. I think sometimes the church is too quick to point out what should be instead of what will be. One of the things the church should do is *practice patience.* As adults, we know how God works within us. As I make my own mistakes in life, I know that I can come to God and know that He is going to love and forgive me even though He does not approve of my mistakes.

The church needs to model reaching out to young people the same way that Jesus reached out and was there for those He touched daily. We need to convey the thought to our church that the God who tolerates us—and I want to stress "tolerates us"—is the same God who is there to love and help our young people. There isn't another kind of God out there who's going to fix their situation. It's the same God we know as leaders and church members. This is the same God they need to lean on, and we need to be just as loving to them as He is to us. Youth can relate to a loving, forgiving God. We need to let them know that God is more than a judge.

The Unwritten Chapter

The church must also understand that the last chapter has not been written in the lives of its young people. Don't sign them off because they have not come around yet. God works with young people in different ways. I experimented with drugs, and I know what it's like to be caught in the wrong place at the wrong time and make a bad decision. I would hate for someone to sign off on me because they judged me because of the past or even because I handle poorly a difficult situation that arises unexpectedly.

There are so many young people who say to me, "Pastor, you know what? I wish my church would just understand that I'm trying, you know, I'm trying. I know there's a God, and I know He died for me, and I know that I can be saved through Him. But Paul had a struggle. He realized that it was this thing called 'sin' that kept knocking him down and holding him back. We're realizing the same thing. But we know that in Jesus we can have the victory. We want the church to help us understand that and then minister to us."

I think this is something the church can do immediately. The church may have to call "time out," regroup, and then get our young people's attention so they can know that the church is here for them and that there's a place for them in the church.

There's one other thing that we need to change. It's perception. There are some people who think young people are all bad. When they see youth, they don't see anything good because the perception is that they are completely evil. The danger is that with this perception, you will never be able to see their good. I want to give you an example. I have a cousin who was one of the first two Blacks to work the trading floor at the stock exchange on Wall Street. (This was in the early seventies.) I went to visit him once and noticed something interesting. During the summer, high-school students were doing internships with these investment firms throughout Wall Street.

Fast forward now and look at what we are doing in the church. We have young people who are members of National Honor Societies. They are listed in *Who's Who Among American High School Students.* They are multi-talented, gifted in every way, and they have so much energy to offer. Yet, while they know the latest computer technology and all the math and sciences, we don't trust them even to count tithe money on Sabbath afternoon. In fact, the perception is that they're in the way!

We should be embarrassed. This is something that we desperately need to change. If corporate America and Wall Street can appreciate high-school students and benefit from their gifts, why can't the church? Our perception needs to change. We need to apply the David-and-Goliath experience. We preach about it, but the church needs to learn how to apply it. Does the church believe in David? Does the church really have confidence that David can bring Goliath down? Again, we know the story, but is it practiced it in every congregation?

Youth are church members too. Sometimes we refer to our young people as "them." No, they are part of us, and we need to refer to them as such—versus the negative connotation of "those young people." Our children are sheep in God's pasture. I am proud to be one who serves on their behalf.

CHAPTER 20

When Youth Ministry Goes Out of Control

by Kim Peckham

Kim Peckham is director of periodical advertising and promotion at the Review and Herald Publishing Association. He has been a youth division leader in his church for thirteen years and is a soft touch when his youth are raising money for a mission trip.

Henry Stubbs could see that things were out of control. For one thing, he was about to put his youth group on a plane to communist Cuba, where they planned to hold an evangelistic meeting. And Daniel— the teen who was slated to give the sermon on the second night of the series, the one who was supposed to hold up the cross of Christ and invite sinners to repent—was insisting on taking a last cigarette break before checking in his luggage.

So, while Daniel stood behind the van sucking on a Camel, Henry could imagine this whole mission trip going straight in the dumper. It wouldn't be the first time.

Their previous mission trip to Cuba had been a disaster. The Westminster Youth Group (WYG) had gone there in 1998 to rebuild an Adventist church that was so dilapidated that the only thing supporting the roof was a rope tied to a mango tree. Sadly, their paperwork had not been as good as their intentions. Barely twenty-four hours after the group arrived they were tracked down by a regional immigration officer. He read them the riot act. "People with tourist visas cannot stay in this town. It is illegal," he shouted. He kept on shouting until ten o'clock that night, and then he ordered the group to appear before the immigration council the next morning. Prison camp seemed like a real possibility, and some of the girls were literally sick with fear.

At the council hearing, two teens gave courageous testimonies about their desire to help the people of Cuba. But the council was unmoved. They gave their verdict: The WYG could go to a tourist town and act like tourists, or they could go home. They went home.

This was not a youth leader's finest hour.

The Holy Spirit and Henry and Arleen

Henry had never planned to be a youth leader in the first place. In fact, he's a bit of a square. He's never watched an Austin Powers movie. He couldn't pick Jennifer Lopez out of a police lineup. The world of most teens was an alien place. "I didn't know that you could act any differently from George Vandeman and still be a Christian," he says with a smile.

Then the Holy Spirit began to nudge him and his wife, Arleen. They noticed that while the membership of the church grew from fifty to seventy to eighty, Westminster never kept any youth in the pews. Typically, the enthusiastic Junior class members would become self-conscious Earliteens, and about the time they got their driver's license, they would drift away.

This became such a burden on the Stubbses' hearts that in 1994 Henry went to the church board and asked permission to start a youth ministry. The board reacted in as loving a manner as possible, while still making the point that Henry was a lunatic. First of all, there was only one youth in the whole church. One single, solitary young person. And second, this was a small church. They couldn't take one of their most active families and tie them up in a hobby-horse ministry. They needed the Stubbses elsewhere.

Well, when the Lord calls someone, He opens the way. After a long discussion, the board voted to approve the youth ministry.

That's nice, thought Henry. *Now what are we supposed to do?*

If youth ministry were a car, Henry wasn't sure where to put the ignition key. He really had no choice but to slide over to the passenger side and let the Lord drive. And that meant that he and his wife were in for a thrilling, surprising, stomach-churning, white-knuckled ride.

The first turn of the steering wheel came when Henry and Arleen were impressed to get involved with mission work. The Lord touched them both with the same burden on the same weekend while they were two hundred miles apart.

They acted on that impression by joining a conference mission trip to Chile. By the time they were ready to leave, the youth group had grown from one to seven members.

"It was a faith-testing trip," remembers Henry. He couldn't imagine where the group was going to find $11,000 to pay for airline tickets and other expenses, but the money came in.

"On that trip the youth really bonded," says Henry. Together they had seen the Lord provide the money. Together they had helped build a church from scratch in two weeks. Together they had seen answers to prayer. When Scott, a non-Adventist who had joined WYG, was afraid his passport wouldn't arrive in time, his fellow youth spent the entire Sabbath School time praying with him. When he went home, the passport was in his mailbox.

The evidence of that bonding came a few weeks later. Soon after their return from Chile, Scott's family fell apart, and he quit attending Sabbath School. Two weeks passed, and then the members of the group—none of whom were more than sixteen years old—determined that they would go find Scott. They drove around Toccoa, Georgia, until they found his home. They hung out with him that Sabbath afternoon, and the next week he was back in church. Today Scott is a senior theology student at Southern Adventist University.

Establishing these bonds, however, led to some criticism. With the vague intention of nurturing the bonding process, Henry and Arleen began Sabbath School by asking each youth in turn, "How was your week?" Of course, this kind of open-ended question meant that the leaders lost control of the clock. Often the teens would open up about personal situations, such as Katie's frustration that she didn't make the school track team, and the class time would be burned up before they even looked at the lesson. "I used to feel terribly guilty about that," says Henry.

When word came to the church Sabbath School council about what was going on, they agreed that guilt was exactly what was needed in that situation and perhaps more of it. So the Stubbses started a Friday night meeting that was dedicated to Bible study. The Bible study goes on no matter what—even if the Stubbses are out of town. "In that case, we have a youth lead it," says Henry. Even the youth who don't always attend like to know that they can.

Late one night a WYG member named Oliver was closing up the Texaco mini-mart where he worked. Two girls came by and started to talk. He invited them to his place to continue the conversation. When it came time to say goodbye, he said, "You know, we have a Bible study every Friday night. Why don't you come?"

Both girls did come. One never missed a meeting.

"At first, I went out of curiosity and was grateful for the acceptance that I got from the group," says Amy. "As I continued to study with them, I found answers to many questions in my life, and healing from many bad events in my past. I continued to go to Bible studies because I needed that happiness that I was finding only in God. The empty void that I felt so strongly in my life for so long had started to dissipate. It was being replaced by a feeling that someone wanted me and loved me *unconditionally.*" Two years later Amy was baptized in nearby Lake Keowee. She now serves as a missionary in Japan.

Henry tried to keep the focus of Friday night Bible studies on Christ and the plan of salvation. Nineteen-year-old Chad says that he learned that "salvation is based on faith alone—a faith that works to carry out the Great Commission of proclaiming the good news." It was this truth that helped him to keep coming back during the hard times and motivated him to become a missionary on the tiny South Pacific island of Ebeye.

Losing Control of Privacy

Arleen is as committed to youth ministry as is Henry. She has to be, because the ministry has made demands on her as a homemaker that go far beyond hosting Bible studies. You can't have twenty teens come to your house every Friday night unless both spouses think it's a good idea.

Sometimes the Stubbses have been awakened at two A.M. by a youth on their front porch. One girl had been kicked out of her house by her drunk mother, who yelled that she hated the girl and wished she were dead.

On another occasion the Stubbses' daughter, Maria, gave a lift home to a mysterious, long-haired junior at her high school. Dropping Travis off at his trailer, she discovered that he lived alone. His mother had moved in with her boyfriend and stopped by only periodically to check on Travis. Eventually, the Stubbses invited Travis to move into their home.

Other youth have also lived in their home for a year or more. "Thirty percent of our youth have no parent in the church," says Henry. "Many of them have not had any father figure—or have had a negative father figure." Henry finds himself being called to serve as an emergency backup dad for several of the boys in the group. And Arleen's willingness to love and mother some of the girls in the group has been rewarded by watching them make decisions for Christ.

Along with the commitment comes the conviction that the youth should be involved in missionary work. But Henry and Arleen's fellow church members weren't so sure. When WYG approached the board for permission to go to back to Chile a year after their first mission trip, the reaction was: "Wait a minute. Haven't you already been there and done that? Isn't there a project you can do in the States? We've got some poor people over the state line in Georgia."

Henry and Arleen kept focusing on something Ellen White wrote: "To show a liberal, self-denying spirit for the success of foreign missions is a sure way to advance home missionary work."[1] Their youth ministry was definitely advancing: WYG was attracting youth from the community who had no roots in the Adventist Church.

When the group got the green light to go back to Chile, they took thirteen youth—almost twice as many as the year before. "We were half the conference group," remembers Henry. "The building project was so large it nearly killed us, but we finished with the joy of watching sixty-five people be baptized." Afterward the youth made comments such as, "Wow, I feel God really sent us here for these people. What would have happened if we hadn't come?" They began to see that God could use them.

Mission trips also demonstrated for them the power of prayer. For example, they were headed to Cuba in 2001, when at the Miami airport the WYG translator was denied entry to the island. "So here are twenty-one of us on the plane with no translator," remembers Henry. "We've got to go through customs without any of us being able to speak Spanish. Customs is severe, and we were smuggling an average of fifteen Bibles each."

This also meant that the group had no one to translate for their evangelistic series. "We were on our knees in the plane pouring out our hearts," continues Henry. "'Lord, what are You doing? Is this not important to You?"

However, the group sailed through Cuban customs. On the bus ride out to the village they continued to pray fervently. When the bus stopped, there was a woman waiting for them. Marybelle Marshall's parents were immigrants from Jamaica who had raised her to speak English. She had just traveled two hours from her home because, she said, "the Lord has put it on my heart to come help you." Marybelle translated for WYG day and night for two weeks. She translated at every meeting. She translated during visits to people's homes. And she translated when the immigration officials came to grill the teens about their work. Marybelle was a miraculous answer to prayer that happened right in front of their eyes.

Because of these trips, a passion for the mission of the church blossomed among the WYG group. "This mission is so wonderful, so incredibly huge," Henry tells the youth. "We have to bear this burden until the last soul has accepted the One who died for them. You are going to finish the work."

It's a statement church leaders make to youth all the time, but these youth from South Carolina actually began to believe it.

A Crazy Idea

Picture the contrast between the youth leaders and the youth. Henry is a clean-cut member of hospital management. He likes to go bird watching and sailing with his wife, who is also a sweet, gentle soul. They are the picture of conservative American Christians. But the youth cast a different image. Some are struggling with drugs or drinking. Some have studs hanging from their anatomy. Travis comes to church looking like Joey Ramone, with hair that swings down to his waist. And some of the girls come in skirts that seem too short to wear in public, let alone church. The youth attending the Sabbath School at Westminster typically lead the praise songs in church before the worship service. With the piercings, long hair, and short skirts, they have at times looked more like a punk band than worship leaders.

But this was the group that made a strange proposal to Henry. It happened when WYG was discussing a return to Cuba after their aborted visit in 1998. The assistant pastor, who'd been planning to preach the evangelistic series, was being called back to seminary. Who could they find to speak? "Why not preach the series ourselves?" suggested one of the teens

"It shook my faith to the core," says Henry. When he finally responded, he said, "Why not?" In his head, however, he could list a dozen reasons why not. *We're representing the gospel. It's holy stuff we're handling. What if we make a laughingstock of the gospel and the name of our denomination?*

They had six months before departure. So Henry gave the kids three months to compose their sermons.

Daniel caused heartaches from the get-go. First he said he wasn't going. "I'm not going to pretend to be someone I'm not," he stated. Then his younger brother, Adam, decided to go, and Daniel changed his mind. "I'm not going to let my brother go alone," he declared.

The other youth reminded Daniel of an earlier agreement. "The deal is, if one of us preaches, all of us are going to preach," said Oliver. "That means you've got to preach."

"I know," said Daniel.

The deadline for the sermons came and went. A few kids turned in their notes. Nothing from Daniel.

This was when Henry really started to get nervous. Things seemed out of control. He remembers seeing Pastor Ed Wright at the Collegedale,

Tennessee, church and asking if they could pray together. "Let me tell you what's going on with some of these youth," Henry said.

Pastor Wright had some wise words. "It's not your problem. It's the Lord's."

Henry tried to remember those words as he stood outside the Miami airport with Daniel and smelled the cigarette smoke. He knew for a fact that Daniel hadn't been off marijuana for more than a couple weeks. And of course, the boy had not written down a single word in preparing a sermon. "I'm not turning in a sermon to you," declared Daniel. "I'm asking God to put it in my heart."

At least this time they had the right visas, but maybe they had the wrong preachers. Would the second trip to Cuba also be a disaster? Would all the hard work and the $25,000 people had given them for the trip be wasted?

One hundred people showed up for the first meeting. Eighteen-year-old Adam preached. The next night would feature his big brother, Daniel.

Daniel was beginning to feel the pressure. He could sense that he was coming to a point that could either be his doom or his salvation. "God, if You're there, show me," he prayed. He had no notes, no key text, and no backup plan.

That night two hundred people came to the outdoor meeting. Daniel stepped up to the pulpit empty-handed. And then he opened his mouth and began to preach. Pausing for the translator, he told the story in John 9 of the man born blind. " 'All I know is that I was blind, and now I see,' " quoted Daniel.

The crowd, including Henry, were paying close attention. This was powerful stuff. Where had it come from? The local Cuban pastor, Pastor Moral, sidled up to Henry and said, "That boy is going to be a minister."

Henry was stunned. Daniel was stunned. Many weeks before Daniel had said that he wouldn't say anything unless God put it in his heart. And now God had definitely put something in his heart, "I was the blind man" said Daniel "and now I see."

The night after Daniel's sermon, three hundred villagers showed up for the meeting. Then four hundred. The kids kept adding more and more benches for the audience, but it was never enough. On the following night, attendance grew to five hundred. "Today, fifty people attend church as a result of those meetings," states Pastor Moral.

The Lord Does the Driving

If youth ministry is a car, Henry and Arleen still let the Lord do the driving. At times it has been a wild ride. Often it looks as if they are going to crash and burn, but then Jesus gives the steering wheel an unexpected twist, and everything turns out for the best. "I don't see many people in the Bible who really understood what was going on," says Henry. "We all too often see only the obstacles. Like Peter, we need to see the Savior and not the storms."

It didn't make sense to start a youth group for only one teen, but now WYG has thirty-seven active members, many of whom are studying in Adventist schools or serving the Lord in foreign missions. About a quarter of the entire church membership is youth.

It seems illogical that concentrating on doing mission work thousands of miles away could help the youth group grow at home. But it does. "I keep going back to WYG when other teens in other churches drift away," says seventeen-year-old Jodie. "I think that WYG is actually striving to fulfill the commission to preach the gospel to every tongue, to every nation, to every tribe, and to every people."

Henry Stubbs didn't know where the money would come from for that first mission trip. As of this writing, the group has raised a total of $130,000 for six different mission projects.

It's scary to have youth show up at your house in the middle of the night because they had to flee from a fight with a drunken parent. And then the years pass, and Henry and Arleen experience the joy of getting a loving email from that same kid who is now serving Christ as a student missionary on a Pacific island.

Henry and Arleen at times wondered why God made them deal with a hardcore dopehead like Daniel, but now Daniel has committed his life to gospel ministry and is studying theology at Southern Adventist University. And Daniel isn't the only wild child who is grateful for what God has done through WYG. "Without Henry and

Arleen," says Brett, "half of us would be in jail, and the other half dead."

Henry thought the first mission trip to Cuba was a failure, but it turns out that the trip was a *good* experience for the youth. They saw answers to prayer. They saw God working in raising the funds, and bringing in huge quantities of mission and medical supplies. And there was one more blessing. After the hearing by the four Cuban immigration officials that resulted in WYG leaving the country, one of the officials slipped back into the room. "I wish our youth in Cuba were like you," he said. "It is possible to do the kind of work you want to do if you have the right paperwork." And he gave them advice that was critical to their future success in Cuba.

So every time Henry and Arleen get the feeling that things are out of control, they try to relax. They don't mind if things are out of *their* control, as long as they're in the control of a loving God.

---

1. Ellen G. White, *Gospel Workers* (Hagerstown, Md.: Review and Herald, 1915) 465, 466.

Fourteen Things the Stubbses Have Learned About Youth Ministry

- It helps to have a name.
- Do something every weekend.
- Find sponsors; you'll need financial help.
- Focus on the life of Christ and the basics of salvation.
- Help the youth bond with each other.
- Engage the entire group.
- Allow freedom of expression.
- Exchange worlds with your youth. For example, go to their football games.
- Challenge and counsel this age group, and let them challenge you.
- Get involved in evangelism so that they can catch a passion for the mission of the church.
- Pray continuously. Pray for each youth by name.
- Be real.
- Don't be afraid of the impossible.
- Never forget that you don't have to be someone special to work for the Lord.

Empowering Youth

by Julene Duerksen Kapao

Julene Duerksen Kapao served as a volunteer in the youth department of the New Zealand Pacific Union Conference. She now teaches Bible, English, and English as a Second Laguage at Longburn Adventist College, North New Zealand.

Looking around at the youth with whom I work daily, I'm amazed that more aren't lined up for counseling, peer mentoring, and personal help. Many do seek relief—in drugs, drinking, and sex, which only sink them deeper in despair.

The awesome truth is that despite all the negative things young people find in this world, there are also opportunities to restore enthusiasm and a sense of self-worth to them. Let me share the effects of two programs that I've seen help young people grow.

StormCo

Service To Others Really Matters (StormCo) was started in the early nineties by a group of high-school kids in Australia. They wanted to impact the communities around them in a positive way. Every year there are many StormCo trips throughout the South Pacific Division.

You know those sad and lonely towns with dusty streets and less than a thousand residents; with houses for sale and no one to buy them; with church buildings with broken windows and no one to fix them; with a multitude of broken homes and hearts and no one to care? We took fifteen young people and "stormed" just such a town in the Northland region of the North Island of New Zealand.

It's truly amazing what getting kids out of their comfort zone does for them. It pushed them emotionally and personally, and it pushed them spiritually as well. During this trip I watched three young people in particular change because of their involvement with StormCo.

Clarinda is a hairdresser from the Solomon Islands. She has lived in New Zealand for more than ten years, but has struggled through both cultural change and spiritual trauma. Her family life is difficult, and she experiences little support and encouragement from either family members or friends.

Clarinda didn't have the money to be part of our team, but she had many of the talents we needed—plus a willing spirit and the desire to go, so we sponsored her. From the moment our team met and started working together, she was the most vibrant and vocal. She wanted to be involved in everything and learn as much as she could.

During our first evening's sharing time, Clarinda's eyes sparkled as she waited for her turn. Energy bubbled out of her, and she nearly jumped out of her seat when her name was called. "I want to be a teacher," she exclaimed, "and the kids think I should be one too." During that morning's program, Clarinda had been asked several times by some of the children whether she was a teacher. She told us that she had always wanted to be a teacher but had never thought she had the skills or potential. That day she had been affirmed.

The night we packed up and parted, it was Clarinda who had the most to say to everyone and the teariest goodbyes. "I'm going to be a teacher," she told us. We'd seen her potential, experienced her skills, and watched her realize that she was a definite asset.

Verity was the toughest of our group. Restrained and quiet, she was observing and at times negative. I wondered how she would handle a week with little sleep, hours running with children, and heavy gardening in the afternoons. She went from positive, to tired to negative, to quiet and reflective. Often, she was hard to read.

One night she came to worship with an angry look on her face and body language to match. I slid over next to her on the couch and asked if she wanted a hot chocolate. She gave a nearly imperceptible nod, and I went off to make one. She guzzled it down and placed the cup on her knee.

"Would you like another one?" I asked.

After three hot chocolates, the frown began to melt and her eyes began to sparkle again. She joined in the singing and shared a little bit about her day during the worship's sharing time.

I found out later that Verity suffers from extreme headaches that affect her moods, appetite, and overall well-being. Late that afternoon one had hit her that neither sleep nor medication could cure. It wasn't until after the second hot chocolate that she began to feel better. With the third, and my presence at her side, she began to feel better about herself, the day, and life in general.

It is so easy to see a negative attitude and write a young person off. Being patient and receptive, waiting for signs of improvement, and re-membering the importance of human touch in meeting the deeper needs of the heart is the key to breaking through.

Verity later asked me if she might help run next year's StormCo for the southern region. Of course I said, "Yes!"

Daniel is the kind of guy that people want on their team. He's a hard worker, easy to get along with, and quick on the computer. He has a quirky sense of humor that keeps teams rolling, and a seriousness that keeps them focused.

Daniel has worked with several of our programs in the past. We chose him because of his desire to participate in service projects and to make new friends. I didn't realize that he struggled with fitting in at school as well as with feeling important and valued—that's not what we generally see in those who staff our programs and youth camps.

On the third day of our trip, Daniel told the group, "Instead of being here for personal gain, we're here to bless the community and those around us. I'm going to leave here on Sunday having left a part of my heart behind." What a statement! He'd found fulfillment in many of our team activities over the years, but none had met that deep personal need to help others. It wasn't until that need had been met that his sense of self-worth began to soar. He was there for a purpose, and chang-ing lives in the community was changing his heart.

Daniel left with feelings of worth and enthusiasm as a young Seventh-day Adventist. He was proud of his beliefs and proud to work on a project where he felt valued.

Teen Expedition

A group of 108 youth and youth leaders of the North and South Islands of New Zealand went on a sea kayaking adventure into the Marlborough Sounds of South New Zealand. There is something amazingly powerful about taking young people out of their comfort zones, throwing them in with a heap of other youth, and then giving them a physical challenge.

The Marlborough Sounds are a maze of bays, inlets, ocean currents, dolphins, mussel farms, and lonely beaches. Our team spent eight days finding their way through that maze, paddling eighty kilometers while doing so. All of us carried our own food and bedding in our kayaks and set up our own campsites every night. We worshipped together every day.

There are a few people in particular who stand out for me—I suppose because I saw self-esteem and confidence building in them over those eight days.

Keri is in her early thirties, an experienced kayaker and a non-Adventist. She came along on the trip when an Adventist friend asked for her help with the less experienced young people.

I met Keri on one of the first nights and was touched by her smile and her enthusiasm for working with young people. She had a relaxed way about her and made the youth feel comfortable. However, I could see straight away that she struggled with her own confidence. It wasn't that she had started out with a bad attitude or was disinterested in what was happening. But it seemed that she wasn't living up to her full potential.

As the week went on, I watched as Keri coached some of the kids in the water. She would move up right next to them, show them how to paddle more effectively, and encourage them in their efforts. Each time she did this, a smile of satisfaction spread across her face. Throughout the week I saw her smiling more, talking more to the young people, and thoroughly enjoying herself. And gradually she changed from being an expert to being a helper and guide.

During church on Sabbath, one of the leaders asked those who wanted to commit or recommit their lives to God to raise their hands.

There we sat on the highest viewpoint of Queen Charlotte's Track of the Marlborough Sounds. We were so close to God, we could feel it. Everyone had a hand waving in the air—and Keri was a part of it. I do believe that Keri, caught up in the spiritual thrust of the week, gave her heart to the Lord that day. There was most definitely an outward growth in confidence and happiness, a reflection of inward change.

Terry is a boy who struggles in his studies and was recently expelled from school. He truly is a good kid; his parents would be the first ones to tell you that. They believe in him and encourage his enthusiasm for life. However, they struggle to keep him focused, fulfilled, and motivated scholastically and spiritually.

The one thing Terry wanted to do during his school holidays was to go on Teen Expedition 2002. He looked forward to every little bit of this adventure. He'd never been on one, so he hardly knew what to expect. Being a young teenager, he didn't lack the physical energy and strength to get the kayak in the water and on its way. But he did lack the confidence to believe that he could make it the whole eighty kilometers from start to finish.

I first met Terry as we arrived at the campsite. His humor bubbled over to everyone around him as he set up his tent and began cooking his meal. His smile radiated to all, and it was apparent that he would add fun to our trip. It didn't take long, though, for it to become clear that Terry had trouble controlling his anger and other emotions. He didn't know when to slow down or be quiet and had problems dealing with the other boys. I could tell that this would be a mission.

Terry was placed in a solo kayak. The first day he did well as he paddled across the bays and maneuvered around tight corners. Eventually, he had to be towed a few times, and I wondered if he would give up because of that. At the end of the day, I saw him crumple in a heap in front of his tent. He was exhausted, distraught, and nearly ready to quit.

Then I saw his counselor approach him and sit down to talk. I'm not sure exactly what he said. Maybe he gave him some praise, maybe some encouragement. Whatever it was, it worked. Something clicked, and Terry hung in there. The next day he was one of the first into his kayak and into the water—ready for another day.

Each day Terry's skill and speed on the water improved. It's amazing the changes that take place when you put a young city kid in a kayak—totally out of his skill and comfort zone—and let him go. It seemed that Terry found a desire to succeed; he discovered his inner strength—things he'd never known before. When his mom came to pick him up, she was blown away with his excitement about the trip. She's praying that the Expedition has helped refocus him. I believe she will be happily surprised.

These are simple stories about extraordinary young people—and about youth leaders and others who are willing to step out and create opportunities for young people to grow in self-worth and self-esteem. These young people found themselves—or, at the very least, grew spiritually—through serving others and meeting challenges.

Gary Hopkins's comments:
There's value in connecting with youth. Resnick and colleagues reported that "regardless of the number of parents in the household, whether families were rich or poor, regardless of race and ethnicity, children who reported feeling connected to a parent are protected against many different kinds of risks including emotional distress, suicidal thoughts and attempts; cigarette, alcohol, and marijuana use; violent behavior, and early sexual activity." Overall, school connectedness was consistently associated with better health and healthier behaviors. And connectedness, whether at home, school, or elsewhere, implies relationships.

See: M. D. Resnick, et al, "Protecting Adolescents From Harm: Findings From the National Longitudinal Study on Adolescent Health," *Journal of the American Medical Association*, 1997, 278 (10): 823–832.

CHAPTER 22

"The Plunge" and Other Ministries

by Roy Ice

Roy Ice is the youth pastor of the Azure Hills Seventh-day Adventist Church in California. He involves his youth in discipleship classes, health ministries, and youth evangelism crusades. In this chapter he describes two ministries that help youth grow spiritually through witnessing.

The Plunge

Sometimes we subconsciously designate certain roles as "pastors-only" roles. Teaching baptismal classes is one of these. Sometime ago we decided to empower our high-school youth to teach baptismal classes to fifth- through eighth-graders. After advertising The Plunge in the bulletin for a month, we began our first class with eleven candidates.

The classes start with a fifteen- to twenty-minute group activity that helps the candidates understand the topic of the evening. Then they go to their "spot" with their youth teacher and have a one-on-one discussion and Bible study as they work through the curriculum materials. At the end of the forty-five-minute, one-on-one session we gather together and have a brief question-and-answer period to cover any questions the groups found challenging.

The Plunge proved to be a great morale boost for the high-school youth as they saw what an impact they were having on a young person's life. At the end of our studies all eleven of the candidates decided to be baptized. I almost had to peel the youth off of the ceiling, they were so excited. They had accomplished something that they were very capable of doing but had never been released to do.

This approach also serves as a great role model for the candidates who were led to make a decision by someone still in high school. When they become high-school students they will have even more confidence that they can give baptismal classes because that is what worked for them. The Plunge is definitely a disciple-making activity for everyone involved.

Wireless

In one of our leadership meetings one of the youth pointed out that we were doing a lot of great ministries but that we weren't doing any kind of prayer ministry. After some brainstorming we decided that we would reach out to our residential neighbors with a prayer ministry.

We decided to meet on Tuesday evenings before dark (people are more likely to open their doors during the daylight) and go in pairs door-to-door asking for prayer requests. I purchased small spiral memo pads for each of the youth so they could record the names and addresses of our neighbors and their prayer requests. We told these neighbors that we would pray for their requests at least twice a day for the next seven days.

Our goal each Tuesday was that each pair make contact with the residents of five homes. (This number fit our time and daylight constraints.) After the teams reached their goal, we met back in the youth room, shared the requests and interesting experiences with the group, and prayed for each of the requests. I reminded the youth to keep their memo pad next to their beds so they would remember to pray for the requests before going to sleep and in the morning when they awoke. Whenever we encountered an individual who was very receptive, we would return the next week to ask how the requests were being answered and if we could pray for them again.

This ministry brought some gratifying results. One Tuesday while we were walking back to the youth room, a white Sentra pulled into the driveway to my right and I heard a man shout, "Hey!"

As I turned, I saw a tall twenty-something African-American man standing next to the car. "Hey." I called back, wondering if there was some kind of problem.

"Are you the ones taking prayer requests?" he asked.

"Yes we are!" I said.

"Could I give you my requests?" he asked.

"Sure!" I said, realizing that something amazing was happening. We hadn't been down this street before, and we were four blocks away from the church, yet when this man saw a big group of high-school youth walking down his street, he knew that they were from the church that prayed for people. There was a buzz around town about our church because of what the youth were doing.

The man asked for prayers for his job, his schooling, and his twins. Then his girlfriend stepped out of the driver's side of the car and asked if we would pray for her too. She wanted to make wise decisions.

We said, "Absolutely," and I asked if we could pray right then. They timidly said OK, and we prayed there in the driveway.

As you can imagine, the youth were pumped that night. They were making a huge difference in their community.

Mike Ross, one of our volunteer youth leaders, teaches computer classes nightly at a local junior college. One night questions about his job and family led to the disclosure that Mike attends a Seventh-day Adventist church. A middle-aged student asked, "Is that the Azure Hills Church?"

"Yes," Mike answered.

The man got all excited and said, "That is the neatest church! A group of high-school students came to my house and prayed for me. They've got something going on over there."

Mike replied, "Those are my kids! That's our youth!"

It doesn't take much for our young people to make an impact on our communities. We just need to lead them to interact in a meaningful way.

Show Them a God With Skin On!

by Bob McGhee

Bob McGhee is pastor of the Adventist Worship Center in Phoenix, Arizona. His church emphasizes meeting the needs of the youth while staying in tune with the older members. He wants it to be a place that can capture the desire of the youth to worship and serve Jesus.

As I was growing up, the picture of God that was presented to me was a God who had a book in which He recorded all my deeds. I knew that the list of bad deeds was longer than the list of good deeds, so I feared that my name was going to be blotted out of that book of life. I just couldn't measure up. No matter what I did, I felt condemned.

My college dean and the physical education teacher at the academy where I started teaching showed me a different picture of God. They introduced me to a God who accepted me for who I was and where I was—a God who had taken care of everything and covered all my faults at the Cross. What a burden was lifted off my shoulders! I determined then that I would spend my life showing this picture of God to young people through my teaching and ministry career. Since then my goal has been to present an experience of unconditional love and acceptance; to show young people that it is safe to be in the church no matter what they might be seeing in others; to show them that "church" isn't a building or a denomination—it's people; to show them that true Christianity is not biased or prejudiced—it does not see cultures, or color, or gender.

So many young people are hurting—often because of their own families. Many are from divorced families and were used as pawns between mother and father. Others view God in terms of a father who is seriously flawed, or vindictive, or hurtful. They want no part of a God like that. They're looking for someone to show them love with skin on it!

Youth need a church in which they have a part; where they have a say in how it is run—a church that's participation-based, not performance-based. It doesn't matter if the sound isn't perfect or the instrument tuned, if they are involved and feel a part of what is happening, then they're there.

We need to show how God would treat them if He were here. He's a God who left His throne in heaven to be with them, so He would meet them on their level and get to know who they are and what they enjoy. He would look at the heart no matter what their outside looks like. He would open His arms wide in welcome and give lots of hugs and kisses. He would spend time with them at the gym after school and would invite them over for a snack.

Music is an important part of my ministry to the young people. I listen to what they listen to and use music in the service that they can relate to and be involved in. Once they see that I am open to their style of music, I can then introduce them to other styles. By finding out who is interested in singing or who plays an instrument, I can involve them.

I've found that when I use the Bible as the basis for messages and use examples that young people can relate to, I keep them interested. I invite them to question and challenge—to become actively involved in discussions. They know that there is no *wrong* answer and that it is OK and safe to question the church and its beliefs. Since I allow questions, they are more open to my explanation, which I give in terms they can understand.

Showing love with skin on it is more than just a one-day-a-week commitment. It requires seven days a week. Phone ministry is one way this can be accomplished. When someone misses church, call him or her. When you hear that someone broke up with a girlfriend or boyfriend, call them both. When you hear of an accomplishment someone had, a basket that won the ballgame, reach out and touch that person directly or by phone. Show your young people that you are interested in all areas of their lives, not just their church life.

Setting up a Web site that has a chat board where they can talk with each other and you about all sorts of subjects is another way to show love with skin on it. Pick a topic that can be discussed—one that stimulates them to think about spiritual issues. Send a nightly or weekly email in which you inform them of the upcoming church activities and share a Bible text. (See the example at the end of this chapter.)

Organize youth-rally weekends and bring in contemporary Christian groups from our colleges and academies. This gives the youth an opportunity to interact with each other and also to find out about our higher educational opportunities during a whole weekend that is devoted to them and their spiritual needs.

And last, but certainly not least, be in tune to their basic needs. Be there to help move, mow the lawn, pick them up if they need a ride to church or other activity, take them out to eat when they are hungry, introduce them to different ethnic cuisines, and get involved in their sporting activities.

It all boils down to meeting them where they are, accepting them where they are, and loving them unconditionally. Isn't this what God does for us?

Bob's Daily Email

Bob McGhee sends a daily email called "Thoughts From Bob's World" to young people, friends, and family both locally and far away. He begins with a text followed by a comment. After that he names as many individuals as he can in the time he has. Asked for their reaction to the daily emails and the Web site, recipients said: "Yes, yes, yes. A fun way to fellowship," and "Yes, all the time. . . . We look forward to it. It's a great thing that he does."

Here's an example of one of his daily emails:

One more from John 21:22 "… Follow thou ME …" Pretty simple … follow the GOOD LORD not anyone else … it is a beautiful thing … Mike Thomas Aser Heye and Frank Lal doing OK … Brad Parmenter … hee hee … Mitzi Abu-Assel hope you are OK? James The and David Knight I am praying for you … Ben Franklin Press and Al and Jan Ghelfi see you folks around … my buddy Chuck the king Watkins glad you are back … Hylands Thompson Lacy Fuller, Bauman Brown(e) and Wright softball in a few days … start running and throwing … Matt Vixie and Keith Perrin you pastors are great … Cheri Oberlick thanks for all you do … Ivan Blake can't wait to see your smiling face … Charli Mattson leader you can come home anytime … Robin Kyle thanks for the note … Dieters you kids are the best … Maurin King Tawny Guenat, Lindsay Temple hope you girls are OK … Jared Branham and Brother Chris Morris and Zach Smith the Raiders will lose … you too Robert Espinosa … :) hi to Walt Meske and Mike Baker, also Bill Gerber and Gary Tetz … time to run out … love to you all … the bob.

Love Is Power

by Jennifer Schwirzer

Jennifer Jill Schwirzer is a mom, singer/song writer, author, founder of Michael Ministries, and manager of Expressly Vegetarian Café. She says, "Having children of my own plugged me into youth ministry. Now I'm hooked."

"From the Christian standpoint, love is power. Intellectual and spiritual strength are involved in this principle. Pure love has special efficacy to do good, and can do nothing but good. It prevents discord and misery and brings the truest happiness. Wealth is often an influence to corrupt and destroy; force is strong to do hurt; but truth and goodness are the properties of pure love."[1]

"How can we get more youth to attend our church?" "How can we keep the ones we have?" "What will make our services attractive to young people?" These were some of the questions that arose at a church board meeting. The board droned on for a while about programs, activities, special events, and worship—all worthy considerations. But it wasn't getting anywhere. Suddenly I was taken with what I thought must be the most original, revelatory, radical idea. Drawing on my experience as a parent, I mentally took stock of what had kept my own kids coming back to church long after the attraction of singing "I'm Gonna Zoom Around the Room" had worn off. As the truth dawned like a blistering epiphany, I blurted out, "Ummm . . . this may sound simplistic, but it's *love* that keeps young people in church. My kids are still in church because of *love!*"

I may have been stating the obvious, but I was right. I had seen it so clearly in my children's lives. It was largely the kindnesses of Christians, melting into sweet memories and melding into lasting bonds, that had endeared the Seventh-day Adventist Church to them. This reality is fraught with questions. What about the mean people in church? What happens when a church is cold and indifferent to youth? What if it can be described by the word that has become one of the most feared labels of our time—*irrelevant?* In short, what if it's not youth-friendly?

God has taken a terrible risk in entrusting to selfish sinners the duty of conveying heaven's pure love. So often we adults get an "F" on the assignment. Yet to be part of Christ is to be part of His body with its members of all ages. He does not present Himself as a detached head, saying, "Worship Me and ignore other believers." Rather, He says, "Worship Me *with* other believers." It's impossible to connect with God while ignoring His people. "The one who does not love his brother whom he has seen, cannot love God whom he has not seen" (1 John 4:20, NASB). This means that in their search for God, the young people are stuck with us.

However, the news that they're stuck with us doesn't have to be bad news. We can work together to present the full spectrum of God's love. No one individual has it all, but if we work together for the salvation of our youth, they will see something of God in us. I saw this phenomenon of teamwork in an incident that happened in our home.

My daughter got caught passing a note in school that spoke negatively of a special-needs kid. The teacher was a very committed Christian lady and expressed her displeasure at my daughter's unchristlike behavior. I knew the behavior was wrong, but I could see that the more the teacher shamed my child, the more flint-faced she became. I realized that the goal in the situation was repentance—sorrow for sin. But my daughter was evincing only conviction of sin and hardness of heart. So I decided to try something unusual.

At worship that night I shared an incident in my own life in which I had spoken harshly about a lady who called to ask me to speak at a women's retreat. Judging by the phone conversation, she was very flaky, and I told my husband so. Once at the retreat, however, I discovered that she was a very smart lady who had a disease that caused her to lose her train of thought. I felt terrible when I realized that I had criticized someone who was already hurting.

I didn't mention the note at school, the child, or the teacher as I told this story, but I could see my child's blue eyes welling up with tears. Then she whispered, "Mom, you know what I said about Tony? I didn't mean that," and I knew that the Spirit had broken through.

The teacher was a principled woman who played the part of the law. I was grace, conveying forgiveness and hope. The law convicted but could not convert, but grace as seen in my own experience melted the heart of my child. Both the teacher and I worked together to present the fullness of truth. At first I faulted her approach, but as I joined with rather than recoiling from her, I could see that what she was doing was an important part of the mix. I volunteered to teach cooking at the school a short time later, and when the kids divided into teams, my daughter invited Tony onto her team.

The Lord of Law and Grace

When the question of winning the youth arises, there are two primary voices that answer. One says, "We must accept them just as they are." The other says, "We must hold up the highest standard before them." I propose that both of these voices are speaking truth. However, we often divide into camps and begin denouncing the voice that does not sound exactly like ours. The "acceptance camp" fires a bazooka at the "standards camp" with the charge of legalism, and the "standards camp" lobs a grenade at the "acceptance camp," accusing them of lowering the standards. The "acceptance camp" thinks the "standards camp" is alienating the youth, and the "standards camp" thinks the "acceptance camp" is failing to impart pure truth. Really, however, it is the battle among the adults that is keeping the youth from enlisting in the Lord's army.

We—liberals and conservatives—need to work together to bring our youth to the Lord of both law and grace. These two seemingly opposing principles really work perfectly together. I saw this once when my bedspreads were doused with chocolate cake.

The house my husband built when my children were babies was indestructible. This was a good thing, as we developed what I call "the answer is always yes" policy. Since I wanted my kids to be in a healthy, safe environment, I tried to keep them home as much as possible. This meant that their friends had to come over on a regular basis. "Can Alyssa, Taia, Becky, Danielle, Molly, and Heidi sleep over?" they would ask. "You know the answer is always yes," I would say cheerfully, and then go home and dive under my covers.

Eventually, a move forced us to sell our house, so the girls had one last sleepover, to which they invited every girlfriend they had ever had. As the festivities began and the house was vibrating with young life, I noticed a chocolate cake on the kitchen table. It had been salvaged from another child's birthday party earlier in the day. I thought about the potential of all that sugar whipping the kids into a frenzy. I didn't know I was prophesying.

About midnight my husband knocked on the girls' bedroom door and said, "Girls, I have to work tomorrow, so you will have to be quiet now." When the shrieks got even louder, I decided it was time to give the girls an ultimatum. My knock brought my youngest daughter out. I noticed that she had a strange, crazed look in her eyes. I also noticed some brownish matter in her hair, and the same substance streaking the tile floor just outside the bedroom. "It's time to quiet down," I said, deep in denial. She nodded and spun back into the room.

As I lay in bed, the voice of reason spoke to me: "Jennifer, that was chocolate cake in your child's hair."

"I know."

"Do you think there would be cake in her hair, cake outside the door, and no cake anywhere else?"

"No."

I realized that I needed to go back to the room and assess the damage. When I got there, the room was empty because the girls were in the backyard hosing off. In spite of reason's warning, I was shocked to see that the room was completely smeared with chocolate cake: the floor, the bedspread, the walls—everything.

I felt an angry bellow welling up from the depths of my soul, "Girls, you get in here right this minute!" I boomed. My oldest daughter came first, wet and trembling. Soon she was joined by another girl, then another. Eventually, the whole group of wet, frightened, semi-dressed girls stood before me with guilt on every cell of their faces. I told them what I thought of their vandalism. I told them that the whole thing had better be sparkling clean by tomorrow, and that if I heard any more noise, I would drive them all home. I also told them that I expected an apology. Then I stalked upstairs.

Clean Again

Now some might say that was very legalistic of me, but it actually gave these girls the opportunity to show how mature they really were when not under the influence of sugar. When I cheerfully invited them to breakfast the next day, I expected them to come giggling and to apologize as a group. Instead, they came one by one and apologized in the most heartfelt way. And they could have eaten their scrambled tofu and waffles off the bedroom floor, it was so clean. The chocolate even came out of the bedspread. The depth of their repentance and reformation matched the brazenness of their sin.

If I lined up those girls and asked them if they knew I loved them, each and every one of them would answer yes. I had welcomed them into my home time and time again, and when nighttime prayers were said, I would kiss them just as I kissed my own children. I had true affection for them and considered them my own adopted daughters. And when they abused that love by damaging the home that had embraced them, they had to hear about it. But the rebuke for sin had been sandwiched between so much affection and acceptance that the relationships survived.

It isn't love that tells a young person that obedience to God's law doesn't matter. Soon the whole world will be divided over this issue, and we want each of our young people to be on the right side of the line. Sinners of every age need to be reminded of right and wrong lest they fall into a state of self-deception. But accountability is a touchy issue for a church that has a history of legalism. We have become afraid of standards because they have been maintained in pharisaical ways. Now we are in danger of letting the standards fall to the dust. If we do this, we will only fail again of conveying that perfect balance of justice and mercy that forms love.

In this age of subjectivism young people need clear, biblical boundaries. To fudge the law in the name of "love" is to fail to truly love. While young people may clamor for permissiveness, most of them have a deep yearning for loving restraint. A study of various styles of parenting revealed this truth. Twin attributes of love—what we might call grace and law, but that this research called "affection" and "control"—were studied. It was found that authoritarian parents who were controlling but unaffectionate produced children who were lacking in social confidence. Permissive parents who were affectionate and spineless produced impulsive, irresponsible youth, and negligent parents produced kids who were more susceptible to substance abuse. It was the parents who balanced affection and standards whose kids were the most well-adjusted. In the words of author Mary Pipher, "According to this research, the ideal family is one in which the message children receive from parents is: 'We love you, but you must do as we say.' "[2]

If the family of God will demonstrate this balance between justice and mercy, law and grace, affection and control, our young people will internalize it and begin to help one another to walk the straight and narrow. Our goal in ministering to young people is to work our way out of a job. I saw this recently when my daughter and her friends began to worry about a girl they cared about. She was making choices they knew would hurt her and others. Like all of us, they were afraid of confrontation. But bravely, they chose to talk *to* the girl instead of *about* her.

They knew that a face-off could prompt a blow up of epic proportions, so first they prayed for her. But they didn't stop there. They went to the girl and asked her if they could pray *with* her. She agreed, and so they prayed again. Then they talked to her about the problem. She listened and heeded their counsel. It really was that simple—an honest concern, a fervent prayer, a heart won. We miss out on so much when we fail to follow these basic, uncomplicated steps.

Prayer Changes Things . . . Like Us

Love has many expressions, and one of them is prayer. Sometimes we wonder why God has us pray for our youth when He wants to save them more than we do. We must pray anyway, because if our hearts aren't changed, we might get in the way of their salvation. Prayer is God's method of stretching our hearts. When we have been doubled over with tears for someone, we are much more likely to embrace them. Those who fold their hands in prayer for a young person on the edge will be willing to reach out to save that youth. And prayer can change our attitude toward someone we don't care about—there's something softening about bowing down and mentioning a name before God.

Like hundreds of other Adventist churches, one small church saw the "apostasy" of their youth. One by one their young members, feeling bored and stifled, stopped attending, until there was just one young person left. Then one Friday night the last young woman broke down and went to a dance instead of a church function. The members saw the same trend beginning in her life that they had seen in the others, and they feared losing her forever. This time, however, the church did not say, "Tsk, tsk, the young people are so worldly these days." Instead they prayed *all night long* for the young lady. In the morning, as, bleary-eyed, they were trying to sing the Sabbath hymns, the door flew open and in walked the girl, also red-eyed from her own tears.

This church was as far from cultural relevance as it could possibly be. It had no youth group, no dashing, charismatic youth leader, no contemporary music and drama. But it had prayer, and it had people who were willing to humble themselves with tears and ask, "What are we doing wrong with our young people?"

Prayer is a boundary crosser. Whether it be distance, time, or alienation that separates you from another whom you care about, prayer can master it. I learned this much more fully when my children went to boarding academy. I hated to have them so far away from me. (They were only an hour and a half away!) I was afraid that they would encounter dangerous influences and become spiritually confused. So I began to pray for them as never before.

One night I found myself sleepless and began to walk up and down my block, crying and praying for my children. Suddenly I felt a sense of peace descend upon me as I realized that God was watching over their lives. My perceptions of reality changed. The stars seemed only inches away, and the whole universe seemed like a warm, safe place. God was in control, and my children were in His hands.

The next morning I received an email from my oldest daughter. I was vaguely aware that the academy was having a week of prayer, but I assumed it would be the routine experience—good speaker, fun time, that's all. The email my daughter sent conveyed something entirely different. She said, "I think something is really happening in my life spiritually. This is different. Thank you for always praying for me. I'm sure it helps in a lot of ways we don't even know."

I learned later that one night during that week of prayer my girl and two of her friends had stayed up praying and talking. The experience began with a mundane conversation but unexpectedly took a sharp turn toward God. They wound up seeking the Lord until one A.M. They were recommitting their lives to Christ and asking for guidance. Eventually, it dawned on both my daughter and me that it was while I was crying and praying under the stars that the conversation changed course and wound up in a mini, dorm-room revival.

The battle is not over for my children, nor is it for our denomination's youth. We are to "put on the full armor of God, that you may be able to stand firm against the schemes of the devil" (Ephesians 6:11, NASB). I would extrapolate by saying that God desires us to "stand firm against the schemes of the devil as he tries to snatch our youth."

Because "the days are evil," we are engaged in a most extreme conflict. But we have the world's most powerful weapon with which to fight it. That weapon is love. And, in the simple words of inspiration, *"love is power."*

1. Ellen G. White, *My Life Today* (Hagerstown, Md.: Review and Herald, 1952), 179.

2. Mary B. Pipher, *Reviving Ophelia: Saving the Selves of Adolescent Girls* (New York: Grosset/Putnam, 1995), 83.

I Found the Ideal Family

by Steve Case

Steve Case is president of Piece of the Pie Ministries (www.pieceofthepie.org)—an organization that seeks to draw young people into the life of the church. He has served as a youth pastor, co-investigator of the Valuegenesis research project, and taught youth ministry at the seminary.

Someone has said that a family is a group of people who have to stay with you no matter what happens. Such a statement makes families sound stable, dutiful, difficult, and drab. Yet families in the Western world certainly fall short of such a definition. Our families seem to split apart as often as they stay together. Even "good families" have children who grow up, move away, get involved in their new community/state/country, and feel guilty for not getting back "home" often enough.

When you grow up with siblings, your image of one another forms early. Occasionally you might update it, such as when an older sister has been away at college for a few years and returns, or when someone has been a student missionary, or a couple years after a marriage. But even if your image of a sibling goes through an adjustment, it rarely goes through something as radical as a transformation.

There's a familiar Scripture passage that says, "If anyone is in Christ, he is a new creation; old things have passed away; behold, all things have become new" (2 Corinthians 5:17, NKJV). Siblings tend to want to paraphrase it like this: "If my brother were to go through a spiritual transformation, a few things might change (such as, he should be nice to me more of the time), but he's still my brother, and trust me, I know what he's really like since I've known him all my life." God may "forgive and forget," but it seems that the best a family member can do is to forgive. Forgetting isn't part of the package. "A 'new creation'? Oh, please. If you knew my brother the way I do, you'd know that just isn't possible."

A similar thing happens as you relate to longtime friends—people who are practically like family to you. Because of your shared history, lifelong images persist no matter what transformations or transmutations occur. "I just can't believe that he's in jail; he would never do something like that." Or "How was she able to nab a guy like him? Isn't he quite a bit above her?" And then there's always the not-so subtle "Don't be so impressed; I went to school with him, and I could tell you quite a few stories." Jesus might have cast all our sins into the depths of the sea, but we seem capable of diving deep and dredging them up again. Perhaps this is one of the key reasons why people move away from their families and childhood friends—it's the only way they can get a new start.

I get to see this dramatically and repeatedly on Maranatha's annual short-term mission trip called *Ultimate Workout*. This particular project targets public-school and home-school youth in the narrow age-range of the high-school years. It's not intended for academy students or large youth groups; Maranatha provides other projects for them. *Ultimate Workout* is meant for those who don't go to an academy or are not part of a youth group large enough to do a short-term mission project on their own.

As a result, most of these teens don't know anyone else in the group. Coupled with the fact that most have never been out of their home country (and some have never been on an airplane before), you have some very courageous—and sometimes petrified—adventure seekers in an environment in which they have absolutely no history, no reputation, no image, and nobody to remind them of such. They all truly have the opportunity to create whatever identity they choose.

Suppose I were a teen on the *Ultimate Workout*. I could claim that my dad is a multimillionaire. I enjoy our Mediterranean-based yacht. Yes, I do get all A's on my report card. And for some reason girls just faint into my arms as I walk down the halls of my high school. You'd look at me with a healthy skepticism, but you wouldn't be able to check out my story. After all, we're in Ooga Booga Land, and you have no way of contacting anyone to get the true scoop on me. I'll either have to live up to my story or change it as our two-week adventure continues.

Most of our *Ultimate Workout* mission trips are to Spanish-speaking countries. I love to observe the social dynamics of popularity on these trips. For example, let's say that on some mission trip I'm Anglo and you're Hispanic. In the United States, Hispanics often are part of the working class, with Anglos as their bosses—a two-tier system. So I might have more expensive clothes than you and start off "above" you socio-economically. But stylish clothes aren't important in construction, and when it comes to interacting with the nationals, I'm at a complete loss, while you become the funnel for all dialogue between the international guests and the local town. My money loses its value and your bilingual ability has gained a higher demand. I must be the pursuer in relation-ships, while you get to pick and choose since you are the one pursued. It's a new world for both of us.

On Their Own

For our *Ultimate Workout* trips we choose remote locations with very simple lifestyles. More than 150 come now, so we divide into multiple groups since the dynamic changes back to American norms when you have more than fifty in a group. With multiple groups we can accept siblings or people from the same youth group and simply put them on different sites. We've had identical twins spend their first nights away from each other because they've been placed on separate sites. Imagine that identify crisis: I'm just me—no longer known as "Oh, you're a twin." We've had children of well-known adults who are no longer "So-and-So's daughter" or "Ms. Important's son." These teens simply be-come "Melanie" and "Jarrod." (I'll use only fictional names for the real people in these stories.)

Since they have a brand-new start, participants can share whatever they want and leave out whatever they choose. For example, someone might include in the conversation, "I make friends easily," but leave out, "I've had two abortions." Yes, that person has been forgiven, but with this group, the sins are only known if she brings them up. Ironically, most participants share more about their personal lives with their new family than they do with family and friends back home.

I remember Janelle, whose younger sister had died less than a year before the mission trip she joined. Janelle came wondering *Is there really a God?* and *Am I as valued and loved as my departed sister?* Although plagued and tormented inside, she didn't show it on the outside, so nobody in Janelle's new family had a clue that she was one sister short in a swamp of grief. During a teen-initiated mentoring group (some teens who created a prayer-and-share group for one session), her first question was answered with a "Yes," which also settled her second question. She shared her testimony the next day—and faith sprouted for others as biblical truth nourished current experience in the life of a "family member" here and now.

Since the new family has no shared history, there is a lot to talk about. For some it takes minutes; for others, days. But because the group has taken up residence in a small town with an even smaller group of North American teens (usually about twenty-five to thirty-five in each group), the bonding together as family is almost immediate. As one participant voiced it, "At home we never eat together, but here we eat together three times a day." The general response indicated a similar epiphany, "Yeah, same here."

Tim had a very difficult background that overwhelmed him to the point that his coping mechanisms didn't include social skills. On the bus ride to our site I was able to draw him into dialogue as long as I carried the conversation and he had only to mutter or nod. It became evident that Tim's responses had been rebuffed, not requested. He had learned not to talk; when you don't engage, you don't get hurt as badly.

But in this new family, nobody knew they were supposed to tell Tim "Shut up" or "Get out of my way, you blob of meat." With new hope, Tim began to practice talking. He started with the fence posts. The next day he spoke to the cows in the pasture adjacent to our tents. Then he took the mammoth step of actually talking to people, although he made sure they were nationals who didn't understand English. Bolstered by an undefeated record of being able to talk successfully and successively to so many . . . objects, Tim eventually attempted to join an English conversation during lunch one day. When nobody shut him up, he experienced a release and freedom like nothing in his life to that point. From then on we couldn't shut him down. He became the most talkative person in the entire group. He had years of catching up to do, and he took advantage of the opportunity. With this new family, why would he want to go home to that other group of people?

On the *Ultimate Workout,* the simple lifestyle we experience consists of togetherness, whether we're eating, working, sleeping, worshiping, bathing, or playing. With everyone having a new start, traditions develop quickly, such as everyone holding hands when we pray. Terms have specific meaning within the new group; for instance, when somebody mentions "the blue door," everyone knows they're referring to the pungently odored outhouse, which has a smudge of blue paint on the inside of the door.

Don't confuse this with the anonymous or fictional characters individuals create in the cyberworld of Internet chat rooms. There's no difference between online and offline relationships here. On the *Ultimate Workout* people live together 24/7. You can't push a button and disappear. You can't walk away or switch to a new or different site. You must live through the experience—a novel concept for most teens. No wonder the intimacy frequently catches the participants by surprise. Tears flow freely and often, as does laughter, listening, and loving. Sociologists would have a heyday with this. For participants, it's a wonderful experience of what people mean when they speak fondly of "family."

Because most of the participants are teenagers and relatively few adults are there, we're dependent on teens to share significant amounts of the leadership. They learn that they are an asset rather than a liability and that they are truly needed *now,* not after they earn a graduate degree and can pull down a six-figure annual salary. I remember our first sixteen-year-old cook, who provided three square meals a day for thirty people while cooking under a thatch roof. I recall the bright eighteen-year-old female who functioned as the construction superintendent for the entire building process on one site. She took aside a strong, vocal adult and told him to back off because he was hurting the feelings of her workers.

Then there was the site that had an administrative staff consisting of a twenty-year-old project coordinator (the overall boss), a nineteen-year-old head mason, a seventeen-year-old cook, and a sage twenty-three-year-old female pastor. When I nervously checked up on them partway through the project, I discovered that their only real problem had been when the thirty-five-year old general staff member had tried to take over because things weren't going the way he thought they should. They merely took him aside, affirmed his talents, and reminded him of his role—and theirs—in the group. That was all it took. I couldn't help but wonder what would happen in my home church if this group of leaders were given the reins.

I expect that those who have never experienced the dynamic of a new family the way I've described it would be prone to be skeptical. Under such circumstances I would. But after experiencing more than ten sets of families like this, I'm beginning to think that I finally have discovered what the family of God is like. I've tasted and internalized what it means to have my mess-ups forgiven and forgotten. True, it only lasts for a short but intense two weeks; perhaps if we continued together longer, we'd end up treating one another like our families back home. Maybe I won't consistently live in this type of family environment until heaven. But I won't be surprised by it there, for I've been in that heavenly sphere, and that's the family for me.

You can contact Steve Case at Steve@pieceofthepie.org.

On Pathfinder and Youth Leadership
by Randy Ruthowske

Randy Ruthowske is a research scientist with GlaxoSmithKlein Corporation and a Pathfinder and youth leader in the Five Oaks Seventh-day Adventist Church in Durham, North Carolina. Myrna Tetz interviewed him.

MT: Randy, you lead the Pathfinders for the churches of the Raleigh-Durham area. I've learned that you don't always do things just the way "they've always been done"—nor even, sometimes, how others are doing them now. Before we talk about that, however, tell us the source of your passion for youth and Pathfinders.

RR: My mom was baptized when I was five, and I started attending Adventist schools in the first grade. I went through the Adventist school system and was baptized at thirteen. However, it wasn't until I was in college that I truly experienced a heart conversion to Christ, aided by the influence of a youth leader named Larry Dalton. I am eternally grateful for that.

After I graduated from Andrews in 1981, I went to graduate school at Indiana University in Bloomington, Indiana. The Adventist church there was small and desperately needed people to fill positions. They asked me if I would lead the youth in Sabbath School and the Pathfinder Club; they couldn't get anyone else to do it. I said, "Sure. Why not?" As I was growing up, my dad, brother, a friend, and I did many outdoor activities that we really enjoyed. Because I had never led Pathfinders before, I did with them just what I would like to do myself—

outdoor things. I remember going to our first statewide camporee. I was surprised at how regimented the other Pathfinders were. We had a good laugh or two over our unpreparedness, but the kids had a good time. You have to understand that even back then I was still growing myself.

Teaching the youth class was more important to me than Pathfinders at that point because I saw it as my opportunity to reach the kids on a spiritual level—to tell them what Christianity and Christ means to me. But Pathfinders and youth Sabbath School aren't entirely different; they are both youth ministries, both serving the same purpose—trying to help kids to see the same Christ that I know. Too often the church comes across with a list of "do's" and "don't's" for children. I think the church is changing today, but the emphasis needs to be more on the Christ who cares for them. It's important for them to know that they should give top priority to having a relationship with Him.

Over the years with Pathfinders and youth, I've found that kids respond very well when I talk to them about what's important in life and about Christ—as long as I portray these things honestly. If you're going to share something with someone, it has to be something you already have. When you have a serious relationship yourself, it becomes more of a *sharing* than a *telling*. In addition, it's important that you be genuinely concerned about the kids. Your concern has to go deeper than the mere feeling that they are a nice group of kids. Many of these kids really crave attention; they want to know that somebody really cares about them.

I think that leading them to Christ is not something you do one day a week on Pathfinder day. You develop a relationship with the kids and attempt to help them buy into what you say is important. Talk to them every time the Pathfinder Club meets. Always have worship with them. When I have an opportunity to have a Sabbath service, I talk to them about Christ. The most important thing is to tell them that there is only one way for them to be saved and that is through Christ. Then you help them to understand how that works, and you give them examples. Keep it to fifteen minutes or less, because kids get really bored. If you can't make your point in fifteen minutes, you probably can't make your point.

MT: Tell us how your Pathfinder Club differs from some of the others.

RR: We meet on Sabbath afternoon. Six years ago Shari Leader (my co-leader) and I decided that we wanted a Pathfinder Club that would provide activities for the kids on Sabbath afternoons, and we also wanted more parent participation. We wanted to make a positive Sabbath statement to our kids. Some of the reasons for doing that came from my childhood. I was raised with a bunch of rules—on Sabbath we couldn't ride our bikes, couldn't throw a ball, couldn't go swimming, couldn't run—so I wanted to change that because I resented that sort of Sabbath mentality. I wanted Sabbath and Pathfinders to be a time the kids would enjoy, and I wanted it to be a program that I would enjoy.

We don't do a lot of class work like most Pathfinder clubs do. We work on a specific honor such as dogs or cats or knot tying, but we forgo much of the other class work. We count on the church school to take care of that, or we send it home with the kids and ask them to "do this with your parents." This gets the parents involved with text memorization and reading. There are other requirements in the class work—such as doing good deeds and helping someone—that we try to meet as a club in our Sabbath afternoon activities.

We have two regular meetings and one activity a month. This is not a lot different from other clubs except that other clubs may spend more time in class. We attempt to make Pathfinders something the kids really want to do and something they couldn't do alone. We have found that the kids really enjoy having something to do Sabbath afternoons and look forward to becoming Pathfinders. The younger kids in the churches are saying, "I have two more years and then I can join."

We strongly encourage parental participation so that Pathfinders does not become a baby-sitting service. It's an opportunity for families to build stronger bonds through doing things together. Pathfinders, then, isn't something the kids do, but something the family does. Parents help with crafts or honors or just details (take care of things that we use, do the paperwork, serve as treasurer or secretary), and it turns out that the kids who enjoy Pathfinders the most seem to be the ones whose parents are actually involved.

A strong point of Boy Scouts is that they require the father to be there. I think that it is really important to get families involved. I've had a parent tell me that one of the best things he did as a parent was to take his kids to Pathfinders because at Pathfinders he does a lot of things with his kids that he wouldn't do otherwise. He realizes that those are things the kids will remember forever. They won't remember staying at home and watching TV—the easy thing to do.

MT: You have mentored several young people. Tell us just how you do that.

RR: Mentoring is about giving your time and resources to a young person. It's just caring and following through as you would with any friend. One young person that I worked with was a good kid. He obviously had a difficult time at home because his parents were breaking up (he was fourteen). His parents and his brother and sister came to our house one Sabbath for lunch, and we looked after them once when their parents were going somewhere. When he was staying with us, I just talked to him about things that were going on in his life. And whenever I saw him or called him, I'd ask how he was doing and then follow that up with other questions.

When this kid became old enough to drive, I looked at cars with him. We picked a car that needed some work, put it in my garage, and then we worked on it sporadically whenever I had time. I helped him get a few things when he was moving from his parents' house and helped him move some items. He's been back to visit twice since he left town and joined the Marines.

MT: I admire your ability to talk to kids, to draw them out, to carry on an actual conversation with them. How do you do that?

RR: It's important to talk about what the young people are doing. What they would like to do. What they plan to do. For real conversations with them, ask real-life questions. Be genuinely interested. Treat them as adults and take a genuine interest in their well-being and outcome. Most young people aren't used to an adult asking them questions that require them to pursue an answer.

MT: Describe some of the other activities you have planned for and with the youth.

RR: Youth dare to be creative. We've done "church on the lurch." We pick up the kids at 9:30 at the church and go to a shut-in's house. We take our Sabbath School program: We sing, study the lesson, and have a scripture reading or a short story. Then we just stay and talk; we interview the shut-in and learn something about her or him. The kids love the socialization, and they find that old people are interesting.

We adopted a woman and visited her once a month. We'd meet at church, jam the kids in the van, drive over to her house, go in, and have our service. Her husband was not an Adventist, and at first he would kind of sit near the edge. Later he said, "Hey, I'm glad you kids came." Eventually, he was baptized. I don't think it was just because of the kids, but I think our visits made a difference.

MT: Anything else you want to say about your ministry?

RR: A commitment to continuity is important when you're working with children and young people. Children like familiarity, security, and stability. If they know the same person is going to be there and ask about them, they feel like it is *their* place. When leaders change every year, they don't feel that anyone really cares about them.

Generally, people who work with the youth do genuinely care about them. It's something we do because we see a need.

Adventist Youth in Public Schools

by Ron Whitehead

Ron Whitehead is an assistant professor in the seminary at Andrews University, where he also serves as the executive director of the Center for Youth Evangelism. He has been a pastor and a conference and division youth leader and has directed three North American Division Pathfinder Camporees.

More than 50 percent of the Adventist young people in the North American Division (NAD) attend public school. Many assume that these young people are not active in the church because they are in a public school. My premise is that this is not true. Many local church youth leaders have not taken the time or effort to pray and plan to minister to the unique needs of this group.

Here are a few ways to develop the involvement of these public- and home-schooled kids:

1. Build a sense of community. In many instances these kids do not feel they are part of the crowd. Most of those who attend Adventist schools know each other quite well and do not feel socially connected with public school kids. Some easy ways to build a sense of community within the group are:

   a. Create social events that will mix the young people. These should be held in someone's home; Friday nights or Saturday nights work well for this. And use events like the Super Bowl, Valentine's Day, Easter weekend, and Halloween as an excuse for everyone to get together.

   b. Plan a domestic mission trip. These trips are a relatively inexpensive way to get a group together: $350 plus transportation costs per person! You'll be amazed at how well a trip in the NAD can create a sense of community in your youth group. (For more information, look up <www.adventistyouth.org> or call 1-800-YOUTH-2-U.)

    c. Get involved in service in your local community. For example, paint the home of an older person, collect food for the homeless, or volunteer at a Community Service Center.

2. Make use of opportunities to become involved in the lives of kids in the public school setting. Many times we visit Adventist schools but don't visit public schools. Sometimes we find the public setting uncomfortable, and we don't know how to reach kids in this setting. But you can get involved in the public school system through the following:

    a. Use the opportunity that Meet Me at the Pole provides. In this annual nondenominational event on public school campuses, kids gather at the school flagpole and pray. (For more intormation: <www.syatp.com> or ph. 817-447-7526.)

    b. Attend sporting events and music concerts. This will show that you are interested in the appropriate activities that these kids value.

    c. Volunteer to tutor kids or help coach the sports teams. If you are unsure where you can help out, stop at the school's front office and ask what you can do.

    d. Support your youths' involvement in student-led Bible studies. Many public schools have these student-led Bible studies. Encourage your kids to get involved and give your support to them.

3. Visit the public school youth connected with your church. Your visits tell them you consider them important.

    a. Visit them at home. Let them know you know where they live. Let them know they are valuable—you took the time to come and see where they live.

    b. Visit them at work. Go by their fast-food restaurant. Have fun with them by giving them a big tip. You'll be surprised at how surprised they are to see that you're interested in their lives outside of Sabbath School and the AYS programs.

These are just a few ideas as to how you can strengthen your impact on Adventist youth who attend public schools. You can find more resources for successful youth ministry in *Giraffe News,* which is a free, bi-weekly email newsletter with many new and exciting ideas on how to get your kids involved in youth groups and how to improve your ministry. Another fantastic free youth leaders' resource are the 411 monthly email newsletters—which cover youth ministry all over the North American Division. For more information on these newsletters, call the Andrews University Center for Youth Evangelism at 1-800-YOUTH-2U or visit <www.AdventistYouth.org.>

More Youth Ministry Gems

CHAPTER 28

Take Them Under Your Wing
by José Rojas

José Vicente Rojas is the director of volunteer ministries for the Seventh-day Adventist Church in North America, headquartered in Silver Spring, Maryland. He served as youth ministries director for North America for more than eight years. Myrna Tetz interviewed him.

MT: You've been very involved in youth ministries. Where did this come from? Did some particular person inspire you during your childhood and youth?

JR: That's a loaded question. I wrote a book on all the mentors who touched my life and inspired me from childhood (*José: God Found Me in Los Angeles*). My childhood was difficult. I came from an addictive family situation with an alcoholic father. We were not Adventists. There was a man named Francisco Madrid, and his wife, Dona Chuy, whom we knew very well. They happened to be Seventh-day Adventists. When my father was drunk and we ended up on some back alley of Los Angeles running out of gas and looking for taco stands at two or three in the morning, Don Pancho (that's what we called him) would come out and find us and pick us up. He would bring us home, and then he would scold my daddy and be stern with him. Yet he very lovingly shepherded our family. I was inspired with how patient he was and what a difference he made for our family.

On Christmas Day in 1968, just as we were running out of food and milk and we had no more food stamps, the Madrids brought boxes of food. It was incredible. To this day it was the most meaningful Christmas of my life. Just a few months later they invited us to Vacation Bible School (VBS). They met our needs. Too often it's easy to judge poor families for their poverty or to bring a box of food and forget about them. These people loved our family, never judged us, brought food, and also made it a reason for explaining the gospel. We experienced the gospel from them long before we heard it explained. You just can't put a measure on how powerful an impact that was on us.

MT: Describe how you became involved in youth ministry.

JR: I went to high school at Monterey Bay Academy, and it was there at age sixteen that I gave my life to Christ. That same year I went out with a team of students to give a church service in Selma, California. I was the singer for the group, and we had two or three sermonette preachers. When the service ended, the pastor came to me and said, "We still have a whole half hour left. You're going to have to get up and preach." I was stunned. But I just got up and preached. I remember clearly that I preached on the cross of Christ and essentially horrified those poor people with all of these details in an unrehearsed sermon—very physiologically correct with the types of wounds He probably had and the gushing blood. It was a gruesome depiction of the death of Jesus. But you know what? I've been preaching about Jesus ever since. After that the team asked me to be the preacher and not the musician. Then, after I graduated from high school, I helped in a local church in Junior Sabbath School.

During my first year at college I was an Early Childhood major, and that just cemented further my commitment to children and youth. My ministry with youth continued on campus. I was a student leader—not elected; I just led in a lot of activities on campus—and I continued to travel on the weekends. By the end of my first year in college, I was sent into Windsor, California, to go door to door and prospect for Bible studies. Within two weeks the Lord had given me thirty-two people wanting Bible studies from the door-to-door visiting. We rented a local Methodist church, and the group became a company within a year. So, youth ministry was already a passion, telling stories, and now making it more and more relevant in local congregations.

MT: During that time you were at Pacific Union College, were there any older individuals who really inspired you?

JR: Yes, David Taylor. He was the chairman of the theology department, and the year that he ascended to the leadership of that department, I was removed as a student of the college because of bad grades. (Should I confess these things publicly?) I had been on academic probation for several quarters. It was Dr. Taylor who sat me down at that moment of crisis when I was no longer a student and I was wondering and pondering what my future would now be. I was still active as a leader and a preacher, and I pastored this church.

Dr. Taylor sat me down and asked me point blank, "Why are you getting bad grades?" I told him that it was because I am a Mexican. I had grown up thinking that Latinos naturally get lower grades; I had no idea that my brain matter could absorb as much as the brains of people from other cultures. He looked me in the eye and in a fatherly way said, "You can do this. You have a brain like everyone else, and God can bless your brain just like everyone else's, and I expect you to use your brain." I was stunned. It was like a revelation. Now I was confronted with the idea that my brain could be stretched. This was the turning point in my life.

I fell in love with the girl of my dreams at college, and it was Dr. Taylor who counseled us and performed our wedding. He dedicated our children. When I went to be a pastor in the Central California Conference, he was the conference secretary, so he supervised my training and my work. He became a critically important mentor who made a major transition in my life in college occur.

MT: During a sermon you talked about young people and their music groups. Then you said that adults need to discipline themselves. What did you mean?

JR: What adults don't realize is that young people are in a growing process, and music styles are constantly changing. Once when I was a teenager I was invited to sing special music at my local church. As I walked into the church foyer with my guitar, I was accosted—I emphasize the word *accosted*—by a well-meaning deacon, who, with a trembling voice, told me that the "devil's instrument" was not allowed in the house of God. When this guy told me that I had to leave, a member of the church board happened to be close by and intervened: "No, we can't throw José and his guitar out." They had somewhat of an exchange in the foyer of the church, and I remember that the one member who had responded on my behalf took responsibility for me. He said, "Let me deal with this situation. If something bad happens, we can explain to the board that I'm the one who takes responsibility." That was enough for the deacon to let me in. I went and sang my song, a very soft guitar piece, and the church members seemed to love it.

I think that illustrates that today sometimes we hear music that we are not accustomed to. Some of the music we may not approve of, but if we would just be patient with young people as they are growing in grace, we would recognize that some of it is reaching someone else. We won't know that unless we test the Spirit, as the scripture says. If it is not of the Lord, believe me, it will not flourish.

As a youth leader in the North American Division for almost eight years, I experienced this many times. Somebody would be frightened by the music being played at camp meeting or some other youth meeting by some group or band. They didn't realize that the band had a lifespan of only two or three months—maybe a year at best. Most of these groups just do not last. It's a time when those young people are experiencing, tasting, learning, growing, and then they move on in their lives. Because we take a snapshot at that very moment, it's easy to overreact and condemn. They move on to things that we never imagined they would, but how can we know where they're headed unless we exercise a certain amount of patience regarding their growth? After all, young people have had to be patient with our music as well.

When you go from one culture to another, the music expression may be completely different and yet the same Holy Spirit is there. The Holy

Spirit expresses Himself in more than one way. You see this at the General Conference session when the African delegations perform their music—it's very different from that of the delegations from South America or Inter-America. The music of Europe is very different from the music of Asia, yet it's the same Holy Spirit. Some of that music is more rhythmic than the other music.

We bring all that to our local church as well. Youth comprise a culture too. They may be the same race, they might be our own children, but the youth culture is different from the previous generation's culture. The flip side is that we want to make sure that our young people never lose sight of the principles that Ellen White had and that are supported from the Scriptures. Why we select music and how we select music is principle-driven rather than rule-driven. If we understand the principles, that is what elevates us to the throne of God.

MT: Describe an experience or two when a particular ministry, activity, or event had an impact, either positive or negative, on young people.

JR: One day I was preaching on youth day in a major church in North America, and while I was preaching I saw the deacons in the foyer escorting young people out. I remember stopping my sermon and whispering to the elder, asking him what was going on. He told me, "It's because the young people are wearing jeans and that's inappropriate clothing. They aren't allowed in church."

I remember leaving the pulpit and walking down the aisle out into the foyer in the middle of the program. I turned off my lapel mike and told the deacon, "You can't possibly dismiss these kids."

He said, "Why not?"

I said, "Because they're your own children—your nieces, nephews, and grandchildren. How can you send your own children home from church?"

He said, "It's their clothing."

I said, "I prefer to have them in church with jeans than at home with jeans on the Lord's day. In meeting Jesus face to face they will develop value systems by which to make good decisions. But if you are denying them Jesus, how will they ever form the values on which to premise good decision making—good, valuable spiritual principles? You have to allow them to come as they are because you love them too much to leave them that way."

He asked me, "Are we going to allow sin in the church?"

I said, "By no means. But please don't consider clothes 'sin' at this point. We want to make very clear that sinners are welcome in this church."

So we went out into the parking lot, rounded up about eleven kids, and walked them back in. Then I turned on my microphone and went right back up on the platform and continued my sermon. That's the type of negative things that I've seen.

But let me share a positive moment that really touches the strings of my heart. There are many positive moments that simply go unreported; we most often hear about the negatives. One that stands out happened at the General Conference session in Toronto. We were training young people in the morning. In the afternoon we went out and did ministry in the streets. Then every evening we had evangelistic meetings in three separate locations in the city.

I had the privilege of preaching at one of the evening meetings. One night—I'll never forget it—a bunch of kids, punk rockers from straight off the street, came into the church with the hairdos, the piercings, the clothing, and the whole collection that would frighten any average adult at church. These kids were into a lifestyle of drugs and what is called mosh pitting. This involves heavy, heavy metal music. You can't discern a melody; it's just a horrendous roar of noise, and they are actually body slamming each other in a pit. They hurt each other—some are bleeding and bruised, and they suffer all kinds of injuries as they slam into each other on the so-called dance floor. Some of these kids were into mosh pitting, and they didn't look at all like what many church members would consider appropriate for the house of God.

By God's grace I made an appeal for all those who wanted to give their life to Christ and take Bible studies to come forward. One of these punk rockers made that step—he came forward! It was overwhelming to see him surrounded by the young people there at the meeting. He honestly wanted a change. He wanted something better. He must have been sixteen or seventeen years old, but he'd been out of the house since he was thirteen and was one of the street elements of the city of Toronto. Now he wanted Jesus in his life.

He went downstairs where we had a café ministry going with Bible study teams who were actively going through the Word of God. He participated in that. At the end of the week, when we left Toronto, we had a tearful farewell. He remained in the hands of good Christian Adventist leaders. I guess we will always remember that young man walking in and seeing Jesus for himself and making that decision.

MT: You're saying that the young people who were working there were very loving and accepting?

JR: Yes. We continue to look on the outward appearance, and it's easy to forget that God looks on the heart. Leaders, parents, adults—we can look into the heart of a young person and see not merely what they are but look deep into their soul and realize what they can become. When you capture a vision of what that young person's gifts can be in the future, then you can have something awaken in you to embrace them and, by God's grace, to burn in them a vision like the one you see. They may not see it themselves. It's interesting to point out that the devil knows the gifts of young people, so he uses them quite well to intimidate us. The more intimidated I am by a young person, the more gifted I realize that young person is. If, in the hands of the devil, that young person can intimidate us, imagine what that same young person can do in the hands of the Holy Spirit and filled with power much greater than evil!

If we look at every young person as a potentially overwhelming gift, then we will truly invest in them and be patient with them. That's why I use that word *patient* a lot. People had to be patient with each of us. Most adults will recognize that others had to be patient with them, but they'll say, "Well, I just don't want them to do what I did." The fact is they are already doing what you did, so remember how much patience you needed other people to show you as a young person and share that same patience with the kids of today. They will blossom. The Lord will bless them. They will accomplish what God prophesied they would. They just need supportive adults and not adults who hinder the blessing.

MT: If you could change anything about the church, what would you change?

JR: I get asked this everywhere I go, but one person really made it a focus one day in a question-and-answer period: "What is the greatest challenge in youth ministry today?" The answer I gave that person continues to be true today: "The greatest challenge in youth ministry in North America today continues to be churches that criticize or condemn their own young people."

If I had the power, I would change our adults so that, instead of criticizing young people, which comes quite easily, they would embrace them and mentor them in the name of Jesus. If they were to take those young people under their wings instead of under their criticism, so much more could happen in our local churches. That would transform Adventism and move us even closer toward finishing this work.

And here's the beauty of it: We have the people. The gospel is already there. The vision is already there. All that's left, all that's required, is that the adults make up their minds to say, "I'm going to do what's a little bit harder to do—take a young person under my wing rather than criticize them. By God's grace I'm not going to encourage sin, but I am going to love the sinner."

The Discipline of Love

by Allan Handysides

*Allan Handysides is health ministries director of the General Confer-
ence. He says that the incredible development he's seen in young people
who have given their lives to the Lord has convinced him that investment in youth pays the greatest returns.*

At night the hospital was visible for miles because of its lights. Set on
the side of a hill in the foothills of the Maluti mountains in Lesotho,
Africa, it served as the major center for health care for a large area. Its
school of nursing was recognized as being superior and was much sought
after as a place to train. Staffed by six physicians, scores of nurses, students, and an excellent business office, it spread its tendrils of care into
the surrounding villages and towns. All 175 beds in the hospital were
nearly always full.

This particular night seemed like many others. Some time after eleven
o'clock I had been called to see a sick patient. I don't remember the
illness, but I had just inserted an IV and was strapping it down when a
dreadful commotion began. The old oxygen tank "bell" hanging from
the tree at the workshop was being beaten furiously. Then came the
watchman's shouts followed by the sound of pounding feet.

Immediately my mind went to the worst-case scenario—I imagined
we were under attack. Just four years earlier there had been anti-govern-
ment rioting, and gunmen had entered the hospital and shot some patients in their beds. Four houses outside the hospital campus had been
burned; we still passed their gutted remains every day. The caution of
one of the teachers at the Mission Institute echoed in my ears, "Some-

times people in these lands can become very excited." Huh! That was nothing compared to what I was feeling at this moment.

My heart was pounding and my face felt flushed, but as medical director I would defend my patients. I ran to a back entrance and roared, "Quiet! This is a hospital!" It was as though a bomb had gone off. Not a sound emerged from the darkness. I wondered if someone would take a pot shot at me.

Then I caught sight of a ghostlike diaphanous nightgown as it whisked between the buildings; next a pair of shortie pajamas; then more. Though the dark skin of the nurses made them less visible, their dainty nightwear caught what little light there was, and all at once the truth dawned: The culprits were not outsiders; they were our own student nurses.

I ran to the dormitory building, but I was no match for these eighteen-year-old beauties. They beat me there, and I heard the door slam shut. They would not escape my wrath though. I awoke my friend Armando, the business manager, who roused sleepily but was far too polite to complain. Taking the keys, we entered the dormitory. We called the nursing supervisor, and along came Veracious Lakay, the matron. We checked and found four of the culprits hiding in the washrooms. I took their names. "See me in my office at 9:00 A.M.," I ordered, and we left the building.

"I can't imagine what would make them riot," I said to Veracious Lakay as she looked at me sideways, gauging my rapidly evaporating anger.

"It could be that they were celebrating," she responded. "After all, it is the New Year."

Suddenly I felt so silly and stupid. Work and cares had kept me from realizing that this was New Year's Eve.

Discipline From Ma Handysides

The next morning a tap came on the door. Four pretty young nurses with rather sullen faces stood awaiting punishment. These were young people seeking to build themselves a career.

I wanted to laugh, but felt that my position demanded gravity. "Your punishment is that for the next eight weeks when classes are finished on each Thursday, you will go to Ma Handysides, and she will discipline you."

"Yes, doctor," they said and left.

The following Thursday I came home tired and ready for supper. As I swung in through the door I heard loud laughter, which suddenly hushed when I entered the living room. There was Ma Handysides and the four students, now looking rather sober-faced. They were eating chocolate-chip cookies and drinking hot chocolate. Obviously they were being seriously disciplined.

By the end of the eight weeks of Ma Handysides's discipline, these young women would laugh and greet me happily when I came home. They'd learned how to make chocolate brownies, cookies, gluten, and sponge cake. They were really great girls.

About this time Phyllis Collins, a nursing instructor, conceived the idea of offering the students extra tutoring if they would enroll in the University of South Africa's (UNISA) correspondence school for a Bachelor in Nursing degree. At the hospital executive meeting we agreed to support this idea.

Phyllis and her stalwart helper, Twyla Reimche, also a nursing instructor, began tutoring the students. About a year and a half later, my wife, Janet ("Ma Handysides"), and I left for Zimbabwe. Phyllis and Twyla continued with the nurses and led the group through to graduation.

Years passed. I became the health ministries director for the Trans-Africa Division, and then moved to the Eastern Africa Division. In 1997, I was called to the health ministries department of the General Conference. One of my duties was to review the status of our mission hospitals. I visited many areas of Africa where we had formerly served.

When the opportunity came to visit the old stomping ground of Maluti, I thought of the ghostly nightgowns flitting about on New Year's Eve in 1980. I looked at the nursing school and the dormitory, and I wondered what had happened to the nurses.

I learned that of the group of nurses coached by Phyllis and Twyla, three now have their doctorates in nursing. My, my, my, how exciting! Matsui—one of the infamous four—has her master's degree in nursing. She married a pastor and now runs a large clinic near Johannesburg. Lilomang, another of the four, married a businessman. Ruth, the third, is the wife of Dr. Boateng Wiafe, the famous ophthalmologist in Zambia.

Sitting in the Sligo Seventh-day Adventist Church in Takoma Park, Maryland, I felt someone touch me on the shoulder. I turned to see a tastefully dressed, refined, beautiful young woman. "Do you remember me?" she asked.

I had to admit I did not.

"I was at Maluti when you were there."

"What are you doing here?" I asked.

"I have my Master's in Public Health, and I run a public health department."

Twenty years. Young African women taken from a rural setting, given a little love and attention by dedicated teachers like Phyllis and Twyla, and a little mothering by my "disciplinarian" wife. How much they, and I, have learned.

The investing of a little kindness, the curbing of pride, the building of loving relationships—who knows what time will bring? So far it has brought me the realization that the potential in a young life is enormous, that young people are yearning to be free, to be encouraged, to be released. Even those with learning disorders do learn if they are encouraged. And it's not a one-way street. These young people have encouraged me.

I wish all of us could learn to support even when things may seem rather dismal. To give hope, opportunity, and encouragement—but most of all, to love. To break out from the chores and the smothering loads of responsibility and spare some time and thought for young people. As we build relationships with them, they will reward us beyond our comprehension with their sublime achievements.

Let's learn the discipline of love.

> *Gary Hopkins's comments:*
> These young ladies exemplify the outcomes produced when people are willing to demonstrate the love of Jesus Christ. We often, as a church, feel that the power is in our message of the Sabbath or vegetarian diet, when, in reality, the most powerful gift we have with which to influence the health and happiness of others is our love, given to us by God. While we should never forget to give our message, we need to focus first on love.

The young ladies in this story grew up in a high-risk environment, with war, poverty, and more, yet they succeeded. They beat the odds. They were resilient. Dr. Emmy Warner, who first described the concept of resilience, concluded the following from research that she conducted in the 1950s:

- Resilient youth were able to reach out and connect with other people in a positive manner; they expected help.
- Children who thrived under adverse conditions had at least one person, such as a neighbor, extended family member, or teacher, who provided them with consistent emotional support.
- Resilient youth mentioned educators who took a personal interest in them as important to their success.
- Resilient students sought out professionals who had respect for them as people, listened to them, and took them seriously.
- Resilient students felt that they could talk to good teachers and counselors about almost anything and these educators would listen without judging.
- Being involved in extracurricular activities and athletics at school and in the community apparently provided refuge for resilient students and helped promote the growth of self-esteem.
- Being recognized for special talents was important.
- Simply being involved in activities that were considered special appeared to increase self-esteem and improve their belief in their ability to achieve success.
- Involvement in volunteer work such as tutoring or taking care of siblings was an important experience for resilient young people.

See: E. E. Werner, "The Children of Kauai: Resiliency and Recovery in Adolescence and Adulthood," *Journal of Adolescent Health*, 13 (1992) 262–268.

The Family That Grows Together

by Bert and Donna Williams

*Bert Williams is a journalist for Sonoma West Publishers in Healdsburg,
California. He worked for more than twenty-five years with Adventist
youth, both as a pastor and an academy teacher. Donna is dean of girls
at Rio Lindo Adventist Academy.*

How can the Seventh-day Adventist Church keep its young people?
That is a question few thoughtful Adventists can avoid. Our own children—Joel, age twenty-four, and Sara, twenty-one—both remain active in the church. This gives us, their parents, reason to believe that we
posess about as much authority as anyone to discuss this topic. And at
the risk of sounding self-absorbed, we will be so bold as to state that we
believe parents are among the most important factors in the choices
young people make about church. Before we proceed, however, some
disclaimers are essential.

The most important one comes first: We do know wonderful Christian parents whose children have not remained in the church. Some of
these parents are peers of Donna and me and among our closest friends.
We're not convinced that we have been better parents than they have
been.

Second—we'll take a little more time with this one—we know that
there are other important factors in the lives of young people besides
their parents. Most of these factors stretch back into childhood.

When we were children growing up in central California during the
1960s, Vernon Bliss was a pastor who had a deep impact on children.
He was full of wonderful stories, he rode the bus on school field trips,

he taught kids new songs, he carved whistles from willow branches. Elder Bliss knew kids by name and engaged them in a way that let them know they were important members of his church.

The Salida Seventh-day Adventist Church that Bert attended as a child had a phenomenal Pathfinder Club led by the Beasleys, Joanna Raffoni, Wally Brooks, Norma Bailey, and others. The impact these folks had on that congregation's young people is incalculable.

When Donna was in eighth grade, her public school teacher, Mr. Mellor, took a special interest in her family. He eventually studied the Bible with them in their home and was a key factor in Donna's decision to be baptized. She subsequently went to live thirty-five miles away from home with Ray and Gracie Mae Howe so she could attend Modesto Adventist Academy. There teachers named Steck, Reiswig, Peden, McConnell, Dennis, and Smith deeply influenced both of us. This is where we met each other, and where we each established our own spiritual commitments.

We are convinced that the wonderful contributions of teachers, Pathfinder leaders, pastors, and others had a strong impact on the eventual decisions of many young adults in our generation to remain within the Adventist Church.

A decade or two later, we were married with children. It was the 1990s, and activities shared with Adventist families—the Coxes, Perrys, Mantzes, Meagers, and Waltons—had a large impact on our kids. For several years Pastor Dennis Farley could have gotten our kids to do anything. Church school teachers—Burgess, Reeves, The (pronounced "Tay"), Kopitzke, Christie, Nielsen, Dull, and Forsey—had a daily impact that cannot be measured this side of eternity.

All these people have been important influences, but when we took on the role of parents, we determined that we would have the strongest impact on our children's lives. While influencing their lives spiritually would not be our task alone, it would be ours primarily. Our parenting always, without exception, took this premise as its starting point.

As important as this commitment has been, however, there is another element that trumps even parental influence in a young person's life. We came to consider this to be the very most important of all factors in all our children's development, and it affected just about everything we did as parents. We accepted a brutal fact: Despite what everyone else around young people, including their parents, may say or do, these young people have the God-given ability—and the right—to make their own decisions.

Not Just Tactics

We don't believe that the question of how the church can keep its young people is the most important question that can be asked. Keeping our own children in the church has never been our number one priority. This is, partially, a pragmatic decision. Young people will not stay in the church simply because adults try to get them to stay. Tell Sara that she must do such and such, and there's an excellent chance she will set about to prove that she *must* do no such thing.

But our priorities for our children have not been just a matter of tactics. At issue is something much more fundamental. The freedom to make individual choices is at the heart of each person's relationship with God. His first priority for humanity has always been the individual's right to choose. On this very point the great controversy between Christ and Satan rages on, with planet Earth as the universe's prime battlefield.

We must accept, then, the fact that young people growing up Adventist will make a variety of lifestyle choices as they enter adulthood. Young adults will not all include the church in their plans. Some will stalk away angrily, hurling epithets behind them. Others will simply walk away quietly because the church offers nothing they find worthwhile. The decision about church is ultimately one that Adventist young people will make for themselves. God extends to them that right, and we must—without passing judgment—do no less. With this in mind, we have focused nearly all our effort toward the goal of enabling our children to make good choices. We do believe that being part of the Adventist Church is a good choice, and so far our kids have come to the same conclusion.

How to help young people make good choices is not a question to begin asking as they near adulthood. The ability to make good adult decisions is a tapestry woven from countless threads of experiences that begin in earliest childhood. Joel is a fine wood craftsman. His oak creations form a major part of our living-room decor. His woodworking skill surpassed mine years ago, but Bert still takes some credit for the fact that this has become one of Joel's most rewarding hobbies. While Joel was in elementary school, he helped build shelves for the living room, a loft for his bedroom, and other household projects. That he is a fine wood craftsman today can be traced back through the influence of good shop teachers to the many experiences Joel and Bert shared together as work partners.

Woodworking is of no great importance in itself, but it serves to illustrate a point: Children become adults one day at a time through thousands upon thousands of interlocking life experiences. Decisions they make in their twenties are influenced by experiences they had when they were five.

Daily home life is so important to kids of all ages. Is home an enjoyable place to be? Is it a place where the kids like to bring their friends? Are spiritual family times fun and nurturing? Are the children respected as individuals, and are their opinions valued even when the kids are very young? Such considerations set a tone in the home that, over the years, has an enormous impact on the decisions young adults make about the direction of their spiritual lives.

We are now discovering that parental responsibility is not complete when children become adults. We continue to play important roles in the lives of both our children because they value our counsel and seek it. They are not required to do this. We no longer have legal authority to tell them what to do. So why do they still seek us out?

Besides the fact that they apparently value our life experience, we think they also value our opinions simply because we have always valued theirs. We began intentionally, years ago, to promote their decision-making abilities. Only rarely in the past several years have we told them what to do. As a result they still want to hear what we have to say.

As this is being written, Sara has just turned twenty-one. "What's going to change now that you can do whatever you please?" Donna asked Sara on her birthday.

"Well," said Sara, grinning as she stamped her foot in mock defiance, "I'm not going to let you tell me what to do anymore! But I guess that's been true since I was eighteen."

Then, after a moment of thought, she continued, "No, it's been true longer than that. Huh—I can't remember when you last told me what to do!"

Donna and Sara discussed this for a while, and neither could figure out when that had last occurred. Bert could remember one time, when Sara was seventeen, that he had given specific instructions to her and her boyfriend of that era about where it was and was not OK for them to be alone together. But by that time in Sara's life, such parental guidance had become rare simply because it was rarely required.

Who's in Control?

From the time Joel and Sara were infants, we made it clear to them who was in control. Initially, it was not them; it was us. We proceeded from a very simple premise: We were bigger than they were; therefore, in any contest we would always prevail. There would be no exceptions. We would set reasonable boundaries, which was our right and obligation as their parents, and Joel and Sara would live within them.

We came to believe in the Churchillian theory of parenting: "Never give up. Never give up. Never give up." Being consistent in child-rearing usually does not require above average intelligence, but it sometimes requires Herculean tenacity. We also learned that when actions of children are rewarded, those actions will be repeated. Simple corollaries follow: Reward appropriate behavior, and more appropriate behavior will follow. Reward inappropriate behavior, and inappropriate behavior will follow.

If the chapter ended here a reader could conclude that our home was a sinister little behavioral conditioning laboratory with B. F. Skinner functioning as chief guru and patron saint. But it wasn't that way.

During our kids' early years Donna was a stay-at-home mom. (Our finances were routinely on the brink of disaster.) She was consistent in her expectations, and the kids learned well where the boundaries lay.

It has been our belief at every stage of their development that just as a game of basketball, soccer, or racquetball is best played within boundaries, so children much prefer to live within a set of sensible, predictable guidelines. If the boundaries are continually changing based on how hard the children push them or on the whims of the adults, the children will get a lot of things they want, but they will not develop a sense of deep, underlying security in their lives. Donna, who has been an Adventist academy dean of girls for the past nine years, holds to this philosophy as much with her seventy-five dorm girls as she has with Joel and Sara. It is basic to establishing deep relationships that have a long-term impact on kids.

Our family has done a lot of backpacking together through the years. You can learn a lot with a pack on your back. You experience an elemental getting-back-to-basics that you rarely encounter in typical suburban living. Most people today can warm or cool the interior climate of their homes on demand. Fresh water flows from the tap even if it has traveled hundreds of miles to get there. The car always has fuel, though it has come from an oil well halfway around the world. Life's immediacy is lost, and with it go some basic building blocks of good decision making.

When kids go backpacking, the layers are stripped away. Choices yield results without fear or favor. Fail to break in your boots properly or wear bad socks, and you'll get blisters. Forget your insulated sleeping pad, and you'll be cold at night. Pitch your tent in a low spot, and you'll wake up in a puddle if it rains.

Pleasurable experiences also reveal cause-and-effect relationships. Toil up the trail for hours, and the reward is a campsite so beautiful that it almost makes you cry. You'll see more crystalline stars in the black night sky than you ever dreamed possible. This is deferred gratification at its best. What could be a better training ground for learning how to make good choices?

Other realities of life also apply. There is, for example, the law that stuff happens. You can make good plans and pack well and pitch your camp carefully, but despite your most determined efforts an unexpected storm can wash out your campsite, forcing you to plod back to the car three days ahead of schedule, soaked to the bone and carrying a sodden backpack. Learning to deal with disappointment is part of learning to make good decisions. Kids on the trail learn that the complaint "That's not fair" rarely applies. A bad situation probably has nothing to do with "fairness." It just is what it is. Not every good decision produces a good result—so live with it. It's not a reason to quit making good decisions.

Of course, backpacking is not the only possible training ground; kids can learn a variety of lessons through a whole plethora of varied experiences. The point is that some life lessons must be experienced to be understood; and these lessons are basic to good decision-making ability.

And parents aren't the only ones who can provide these experiences. Joel and Sara benefited from adventures with other adults—teachers, pastors, other parents. We didn't raise our kids alone, and we enjoyed opportunities to provide good experiences for other peoples' kids too. However, only parents have the sustained, long-term relationship with children that allows them to make the development of decision-making skills a primary objective. It is rarely possible for anyone else, no matter how well meaning, to fill this role.

As the years went by, Joel and Sara did give increasing evidence that they were capable decision makers. The control that we had worked so tenaciously to exert when they were small had, increasingly, become their own self-control. There was a transition taking place: Parental discipline was decreasing; self-discipline was on the rise. As their teenage years progressed, Joel and Sara needed our direct guidance less and less, and by their later teens it was largely beside the point.

We believe that Joel's and Sara's ability to make good choices has contributed to the decisions they've made to remain a part of the Adventist Church. We have never told them that's what they should do. But we do think our family's experience together over the years has had an impact on these decisions.

We've hesitated to offer the thoughts contained in this chapter. It can easily sound like gloating—you know, "We have good kids, and you don't." Please—that is not the point. We also hesitate because we cannot claim with certainty that our children will remain in the church. They are still young and are still working through some of their most important decisions.

As this is being written our children and some of their friends are deeply engaged in an ongoing conversation about what it means to be Christians and Adventists. Personal spirituality is a high priority for them. In a recent conversation Joel asked us, "What is more important than this?"

But they are not just comfortably sliding into the pews in their local churches. They are asking probing questions—sometimes unsettling questions. Where is the church headed? Does the church actually know where it is headed? Do they feel drawn by their own deep convictions to the place where the church is headed?

We are gratified that Joel and Sara continue to engage us in long conversations about spiritual life and about the church. Our goal has always been to provide them with skills that enable this process. It has now become a process that deeply challenges our own thinking.

Gary Hopkins's comments:

A few years ago some interesting research emerged on decision making during adolescence. In a nutshell, this research revealed that youngsters whose parents allow them to become involved in the decision-making matters of the home are more likely to take on the values of the parents. So get your kids involved in making decisions early. But don't expect perfection, because they probably won't see perfection in you.

See: S. B. Silverberg and D. M. Gondoli, "Autonomy in Adolescence: A Contextualized Perspective," in G. R. Adams; R. Montemayor; and T. P. Gullotta, eds., *Psychosocial Development During Adolescence: Progress in Developmental Contextualism* (Thousand Oaks, Calif.: Sage Publications, 1996), 12–61.

C H A P T E R 3 1

Living Beyond Statistics

by Bonita Joyner Shields

Bonita Joyner Shields served as an associate pastor of the Spencerville Seventh-day Adventist Church before joining the staff of the Adventist Review *as an assistant editor. She lives in Brookeville, Maryland, with her husband, Roy.*

If my life were determined by statistics, I would most likely be a high-school dropout who married an abusive alcoholic and was now forging a career at McDonald's. But statistics have not determined my life. God cannot be bound by them. While I don't profess to understand how God works in individuals' lives, I do know that He has directed in my life since I was a child. And He did it most visibly through His people—the church.

Mom and Dad married in 1951. Neither had ever heard of Seventh-day Adventists before Mrs. Brownell, a Bible worker, meandered through town. Mrs. Brownell came to the door and asked my paternal grandmother (whom my parents were living with at the time) if she would like to take Bible studies. My grandmother initially said Yes but decided at the last minute that she didn't want to take the studies, so my parents took them instead. Mom and Dad joined the Seventh-day Adventist Church in 1955. Mrs. Brownell nurtured them in the faith. To this day my mom quotes Mrs. Brownell on varied topics.

Eventually, four children came along. I, being the youngest, was born in 1963. My mom was a stay-at-home mom. Dad worked as an electrician to support the family. He served as a deacon in the church, and Mom helped with Dorcas. We were your typical Adventist family.

But I'm sure it was just as tough physically and financially to raise a family of four in the early 1960s as it is today. You know how it is by the end of the week: Exhaustion sets in. All you can think about doing is relaxing. My parents started their downward spiral by staying away from church. Then comments from church members took their hold.

When times get tough, we tend to fall back on those survival mechanisms that we learn early in life. My dad's father chose to kill his pain through alcohol. My mom's parents used that same method. Dad had stopped drinking when he and Mom got married, but alcohol is a "friend" that isn't hard to find after years of absence. Then one Christmas Eve Mom started drinking too.

On Sabbaths after Mom and Dad stopped going to church, I would dress myself, stand on the curb, and wait expectantly for Uncle Fred to pick me up and take me there. Uncle Fred and Aunt Kitty, Dad's sister, were the only other Adventists in either Dad's or Mom's families. Dad had given them Bible studies and brought them into the church.

Uncle Fred and I would take the scenic route to church along the Chesapeake Bay while I drove. (Well, as much as a six-year-old can drive.) Actually, I would sit on Uncle Fred's lap and steer while he worked the pedals. When we arrived at church, all the kids would run to the car because they knew what Uncle Fred kept in his glove compartment: butterscotch candies!

There was just something about Uncle Fred that made children love him—that made *me* love him. I knew my parents loved me. But every kid needs an Uncle Fred—someone outside of those who are "supposed" to love us. Someone who loves us with time and acceptance.

Church became a pivotal part of my life at an early age. Church was fun. Church was stability. Church was the peace and calm in the midst of chaos.

Suspended

I was a good kid. Even my brothers and sisters thought so; which is why it was quite a shock for them when I got suspended from school in fifth grade.

Why did we have to wear such long skirts?

The teachers made us stand straight and place our arms firmly against our legs. The length of our longest finger was the guide for the length of our skirts. *Ridiculous!* At least that's what my girlfriends and I thought.

One particular fall day, we decided that we'd had enough. We all wore skirts with elastic waistbands to school. When we arrived at school that morning, we rolled our skirts up at the waist to make them shorter. (As if the teacher wasn't going to notice!) There—we were *cool!*

It didn't take long for the teacher, who also happened to be the principal, to call us into his office. Mr. Kriigle was a soft-spoken, fun-loving guy. We all liked him. He was actually being quite kind to us as he spoke with us about our skirts. I don't think he was going to suspend me, but I gave him no other option.

As I said before, I was a pretty good kid. But I had an Achilles' heel: my smart mouth. As Mr. Kriigle was talking with me about the skirt, I looked at him and replied quite sarcastically, "Well, if you want me to wear different clothes, why don't you go out and buy them for me yourself?"

When Mom brought me home from school that day, Dad and the rest of the family were outside. Mom told them what had happened, and they were incredulous. "No, not Bonita!" "You *are* kidding, aren't you?" I think they were getting a kick out of the situation.

Dad wasn't amused though. He didn't say much that day; he was too angry. When he did finally speak, he spoke slowly and weighed his words carefully. "Do you know the only reason you are at that school?"

I may have had a smart mouth, but I wasn't dense. I kept my mouth shut this time.

"Because the church helps pay your bill."

It took a lot for a father to admit to his young daughter that he was dependent on church funds to send her to church school. It also knocked a large part of the chip off my shoulder. Major attitude adjustment; no spanking required.

By the end of my sixth-grade year, my two brothers and my sister had begun going to public school. "Not fair!" I cried. Despite my attitude adjustment I wanted to get out of church school and go to public school. I was tired of wearing dresses to school. I was tired of going by their rules. I was tired of all the clichés. And today my thirty-nine-year-old woman's understanding says that I was also tired of feeling like an outcast.

I did gain my "freedom" in seventh grade and went to public school. My first emancipation act was to not wear dresses the entire seventh-grade year. Along with my "breaking out" of church school I decided I was also tired of all the hypocrites, so I also broke out of the church.

I began attending the Episcopal church with my eldest brother, Ben. I attended the youth groups. I sang in the choir. And at the age of twelve I became one of their first female acolytes. (An acolyte is someone who, among other things, carries the cross during the processional and assists with the offering and Communion.) I became disenchanted with the Episcopal church when I discovered they weren't perfect. Even they had hypocrites.

I then began attending the Church of the Nazarene with my other brother, Bruce. What a caring and compassionate group of people. They accepted me—with my worship attire of blue jeans and the *smaller* chip on my shoulder.

My brother hung around with the Baine kids. There were at least eight kids in that family. They were *everywhere!* But it was seventeen-year-old Mark, who wore a ponytail and had a foot with six toes, whom I remember most. He's the one who would sit with me on the living-room floor and share with me about how the Lord brought him from a life of drugs. He's the one who so lovingly convinced me that I didn't have to wear three inches of make-up to look beautiful. And he's the one who, kneeling on that same living-room floor, guided me to accept Jesus as my Lord and Savior.

The Church of My Youth

Hampton Roads Seventh-day Adventist Church: 1977. An evangelist, David Green, was in town. Mom and Dad wanted to go, so I went with them.

David Green wasn't your typical dynamic, extrovert of an evangelist. He was soft-spoken—but not weak. He held convictions, but he wasn't going to knock you over the head with them or tire you out with his hyperactivity. He was going to "reason together."

What was it that night that compelled me to go down to the front of the sanctuary for the altar call? Was it the sentimental mood of being in my childhood church again? Was it peer pressure? Or parental pressure? No. It was the heart-change of having truly accepted Jesus as my Savior and Lord plus the realization that no church is perfect. No person is perfect. All churches have hypocrites, and I contribute my share to the hypocrisy heap. While I found godly people in those other churches I attended, and while God was leading me in those churches just as much as He is leading me today, I discovered that *my* church, the church of my childhood, understands the character of God like no other.

The very night I returned to the church of my youth I determined that I would attend Shenandoah Valley Academy (SVA). Why was I so determined? I think the guy wearing the white sheet had something to do with it.

I attended public school at the height of integration; therefore, we did not attend schools in our neighborhoods, but were bussed across town. I really don't blame the Blacks in that neighborhood for resenting the White folks invading their territory. But their resentment resulted in acts of violence. White teachers were jumped in back hallways. White students were thrown down steps. I stayed away from bathrooms for fear of being assaulted. (Try going an entire day without using a bathroom.)

I became quite adept at acting tough. Being tall helped. I would hold my head back, look down my nose, and never smile. I looked quite intimidating. Beneath the tough façade, however, I was terrified. I came home each day and wept while sitting at the dinner table. But the day I saw the Ku Klux Klan guy standing across the street dressed in a white sheet, watching our school, clinched it for me. It was going to get messy. I had to get out.

I attended SVA for the last three-and-a-half years of high school and thought I had gone to heaven! Why? Is boarding academy perfect? No. I had a rough start—hung out with the wrong crowd, entered an emotionally abusive dating relationship, and grieved the

death of a friend by drugs. But I ultimately found what I was looking for. I was looking for a safe place to find counselors to lead me,
friends for life, and role models for my Christian walk. And I found
them all.

The summer after my freshman year my parents were unsure as
to whether they could afford to send me back the following school
year. I remember sitting next to my dad, asking despondently,
"Daddy, am I going to be able to go back to SVA?" Daddy held me
and replied, "Nita, we're not putting our money into pockets with
holes in them. We're putting it into a bank that will last through
eternity."

I graduated from SVA with a bill of $25. How?

Through the sacrifices of my parents. By the grace of God, they had
quit drinking a few years before, but they were still trying to recover
financially from those lost years. To keep me in this Christian boarding
academy, they went without basic furniture and other needs. (My Aunt
Kitty would also buy me clothes occasionally, and—though she probably wouldn't admit it—I think also contributed money to my school
account.)

Through my working. I held jobs during the school year and each
summer. I began my high-school boarding career as a janitor in the
girls' dorm. By my senior year I had become the principal's secretary. I
treasure my education because I invested so much of myself in it. Nothing worth having comes easily.

And because of my church. Without the Worthy Student Fund, I would
not be a graduate of Shenandoah Valley Academy. I would probably be
hanging around with my public school friends, and lacking focus in
life.

Job or College?

The summer after I graduated found me working as a clerk/typist at
the Newport News Shipyard (where my parents also worked). Since
Mom's and Dad's jobs required them to be at work thirty minutes before mine did, they dropped me off early. That allowed me time to have
my worship before my co-workers arrived.

Since my cubicle didn't have a door, many times the early birds walking by would engage me in conversation when they discovered what I was doing. One big, burly fellow loved to draw me into discussions of controversial topics. I also enjoyed some nice, spiritual talks with a grandfatherly-type who would stop by. I told him I was planning to attend a Christian college that fall. I also told him I wanted to marry a Christian guy. He looked at me quizzically and asked, "How do you know you will marry a Christian? Doesn't it depend on who you fall in love with?"

I replied, "Well, I guess I'll just have to date Christian guys!" We went around and around on this topic, but he couldn't quite grasp the idea that we had a *choice* in whom we married.

At the end of the summer, my supervisor called me into his office. He asked me if I wanted to stay and become the supervisor for their data-processing department. I considered it a compliment to my abilities and also to the principles instilled through a Christian education. I didn't have to think for long, though. I wasn't going to give up my dream. I was going to college!

My church members thought I had lost my marbles. "Columbia Union College? Why do you want to go *there?*" Some referred to it as Sin City. They thought other denominational schools had a much more "spiritual" atmosphere. (In other words, they were located out in the boonies where nothing bad could find you.)

My response to them was, "The kingdom of God is *within* you."

I attended CUC and again found what I was looking for—wise, godly counselors; role models for my Christian journey; and a Christian partner for life.

More and more Adventists are choosing public education. I think if they live by the philosophy, "The kingdom of God is within you," they can provide a tremendous Christian witness on their high-school or college campuses.[1] My choice, however, was the best for me. My education is a part of me that I cherish deeply. I believe the purpose of education is not merely to instill knowledge, but also to instill desires and capabilities to serve our fellow human beings in the name of Christ.

I have always felt a kinship with the prophet Samuel. Not that I am a prophet or the daughter of a prophet! But I can relate to him regarding the role that God's house played in his life from an early age.

I feel most at home at church. Not that I don't venture from home and out into the world. But when I sit in God's house, among God's people, I feel a sense of belonging, of completion.

God's house is where I find definition for my life.

God's house is where I find healing for the wounds that sin brings to us all in this world. God's house is where I find strength to live beyond statistics.

------

1. See John Van Eyk, "The Influencing of Searching Minds: How to Make a Public College Student Feel Part of the Church," *Adventist Review*, June 20, 2002.

Gary Hopkins's comments:

Many Seventh-day Adventist schools are places where students experience a high sense of community. The term "Christian education" implies an environment of caring and love, of cooperation and celebration of Christian beliefs.

Our schools face special challenges because they are supported by constituent churches. Members of these constituencies may be tempted to take ownership by placing their personal demands on the school. Then tensions build, and teachers may be driven to switch their church membership to nonconstituent churches or to move on to the public educational system.

None of this even starts to fit into what we know schools need in order to provide the best in Christian education. Rather than disagreeing with these schools and complaining, we would be much wiser to get involved by spending two or three hours each week at school to help students think of their school as a functional community.

Let's get involved.

—Adapted from *It Takes a Church* (Nampa, Idaho: Pacific Press®, 2002), chapter 7.

Personal Preparation

Grace and the Twelve-Step Group

by Jackie Bishop

Jackie Bishop is children's ministries director for the Rocky Mountain Conference, a REAL learning specialist, and a cowriter for GraceLink. *She says her greatest claim to fame remains the raising and homeschooling of Jesse, seventeen, Cheyenne, fifteen, and Cassidy, eleven.*

"Hi. My name is Jackie. I'm a recovering sinner."

Being part of a twelve-step recovery program was not something I envisioned in college, but God has begun to change my life radically. I just celebrated twelve months practicing the program.

At each meeting we go around the circle and introduce ourselves by our first name and admit our dependency. Everyone else responds to my introduction in unison, "Hi, Jackie!" Whatever my problems, with the group I am not invisible, not alone—I am accepted and have support.

Here I learn to pray the Serenity Prayer:

God, grant me
The serenity to accept the people I cannot change,
The courage to change the person I can, and
The wisdom to know that person is me.

The most incredible gift I have received from this program is a touchable, tangible, experience of grace in action at every meeting, every time I attend. Because I am the adult child of addicted parents and grandparents, I desperately need the support that Al-Anon offers me.

I wish I had found twelve-step groups long ago, but denial is one of our favorite coping mechanisms. So it wasn't until last year that I admitted to being a very accomplished enabler in need of Al-Anon, a program for friends and families of alcoholics, and Nar-Anon, a support program for friends and families of drug addicts.

I have experienced more grace and acceptance in these meetings than in all my lifetime of other classes and meetings. At a twelve-step meeting I get to talk about whatever is on my mind. I can talk about stuff that is bothering me and what I think I should do about it. What I say might be judgmental or the solution to the problem I raise may be as obvious to everyone else as the nose on my face. But nobody puts me down; nobody tells me what to do. Instead I am loved and supported until I finally figure out that I cannot change the person or problem; I can change only myself. Which, if you think about it, is just what God does. In a book about providing an atmosphere of love, acceptance, and protection for our kids, we need to talk about mentoring kids with grace, using the amazing principles of the twelve-step program.

True North

When speaking to people about the need to teach children with grace, I often ask everyone to close their eyes and point due north. We then keep pointing as we open our eyes. Everyone is pointing in a different direction. It occurs to me that one of the reasons we seem to have difficulty providing our kids with the safe teachable environment we want them to have is that lots of us are unsure exactly which direction to point them. We so desperately want to effect the outcome that we forget that our job is to lift Jesus up and that it's *His* job to draw them! Only after experiencing God's drawing power will kids begin to understand what attracts them to Him. Only then will they value His plan for their lives.

We have a slogan in twelve-step arenas: *There is One God, and you are not He.* This slogan reminds me to give careful thought and consideration to what is and what is not my responsibility. A story is told of a young child who desperately wants to help her dad with the backyard fence. Needing first to go to the store for supplies, the father leaves her to clean up around the fence. When she has finished her assigned task before he returns, she decides to help further. With an old paintbrush and some leftover paint, she begins the tedious job of painting the old fence.

On his return, her dad, seeing her messy attempt, quickly affirms her desire to be helpful. Then he announces that he has good news and bad news. The bad news is that he is planning to tear down the fence—that is why he went to the store for building supplies. The good news is that she will get to help him replace the fence, and this time she'll be working with his expertise, new tools, and fresh paint. Together they build a new fence, perfect for their yard and needs.

There was no other way this child could have been successful; the job was not hers, the tools were damaged, and only her father was capable of achieving the goal. We who minister to children must focus on what God is calling us to do. As the Serenity Prayer suggests, we can change only *our* choices, *our* reactions, and *our* behavior. Everything else we must accept and leave entirely to God, which for some of us is easier said than done—hence the need for twelve steps.

Twelve Steps for Recovering Sinners Who Minister to Children

The originators of the twelve-step program worded their steps so as to describe the process of recovery that had worked for them. What follows is my suggested revision of these steps as a set of principles for recovering sinners who minister to children.

Steps 1-3

The first three steps help us clarify our responsibility in relation to God's responsibility:

1. We admitted we were powerless over sin and that our lives had become unmanageable.

In other words, I am completely unable to fix, correct, rebuild, mold, save, restore, rescue, or save any other person, including the children in my life. Focusing on any of these salvation efforts tends to drive people crazy, generally messing up their lives.

2. Came to believe that a Power greater than ourselves could restore us to sanity.

Remembering that there is a God and that He has no grandchildren has been a huge comfort to me and has changed my focus and the direction of my ministry to kids. God is big enough to accomplish His will in the lives of kids with or without me. He allows me the privilege of being a small part of His recovery plan. When I leave His job to Him, I am much saner and a much safer shepherd for His children.

3. Made a decision to turn our will and our lives over to the care of God as we understood Him.

I love that this step says "made a decision to . . ." because often I cling to my need to be in control and to effect my outcome. So I constantly make the decision to submit to the will of God. I continue to pray, "God, You know what these kids need to hear, see, and experience. I am an empty vessel for Your use."

The program says of these first three steps: We came, we came to, and we came to believe. To me they mean: I *arrived* at the foot of the cross completely needy, I *came to* an awareness of who God is and who I am, and then I *began to really believe* that He is big enough to handle my needs perfectly, so I can surrender them to Him.

Three twelve-step slogans that correspond to these first three steps might be useful in your home or church situation: "One day at a time." Each day is a brand-new opportunity to start over, to remind myself once again of my calling and God's plan for my life and the lives of those around me. I hope I can always remember that this slogan applies to children as well as to me.

"Easy does it." I need this slogan when I start to panic because things are not going my way—when the kids around me are making poor decisions or at least ones that I don't agree with. When I want to put on my God robe, "easy does it" reminds me that it's God's job, not mine, to fix and save people. My part is to love, support, nurture, and accept them while God is doing His work.

"This too shall pass." Many things look bigger than they really are. That's when I need to remember God is in charge; He alone knows what the future holds. The waiting time goes better when I keep focused on what God has called me to do—to lift Him up so He can draw the children and their families to Himself.

Steps 4-7

The next four steps remind me that God's job is to fix and to change; my job is to depend, submit, and serve. I must keep my primary focus on myself and my need to constantly seek God's care, guidance, and forgiveness in my life. They help me focus on being real, on being honest, and on being relational. When I practice these three steps, I am accepting and accountable; I can create a safe, honest place for kids to come and be themselves.

4. Made a searching and fearless moral inventory of ourselves.

Keeping the focus on my growth in Jesus is the key element here. The temptation is to look outside myself and take inventory of others, especially children and youth. Their defects, weaknesses, and sins are an easy target. The danger is that I will become so focused on fixing others that I have little or no time to seek God's examination of my own heart and behavior. However, I have discovered that when I seek to maintain the vertical relationship between myself and God, the horizontal relationship I have with others naturally lines up as well.

5. Admitted to God, ourselves, and to another human being the exact nature of our wrongs.

Eugene Petersen, in his book *Like Dew Your Youth,*[1] suggests that parents and teachers "engage in vigorous Christian growth on their own and permit their children to look over their shoulders while they do it." Parents don't have to be perfect, but they must admit that they are "growing up in Christ. They must do it openly before adolescents so that the adolescents can observe, imitate, and make mistakes in the context of care and faith."

Petersen further maintains that one of the best models for mentoring is the concept of apprenticeship. "The young apprentice is placed in close association with a master for a period of years. Through the association a discipline is shared, skills are acquired, the work discussed. The master is seen at his best and worst. The master allows himself to be vulnerable to the apprentice, who sees him make mistakes and how he reacts to his mistakes."

6. Were entirely ready to have God remove all these defects of character.

When our children see us admitting our weaknesses and admitting the challenges and pain they cause, they are more likely to "catch" the values that we so desperately want them to possess for themselves.

7. Humbly asked Him to remove these shortcomings.

We continue to focus on how God is creating within us a new heart. What comes from this brand-new heart can only be His will for the children within our influence.

Steps 8-10

The next three steps are about giving back—helping someone else climb the ladder behind us. Homes and churches can help kids understand what their job is and create a grace-filled environment in which they can learn to live consistent lives of grace and obedience. The teacher's challenge is to model forgiveness, to let the kids see what it looks like and sounds like to be constantly tuned in to the Father's will.

8. Made a list of all persons we harmed and became willing to make amends to them all.

The hardest prayer for most of us to pray is the part where we make confession of our wrongs. Perhaps when we come to this part of our evening prayers we should take up pencil and paper and make a list of those we may have harmed that day, not forgetting the children in our lives.

9. Made direct amends to such people wherever possible, except when to do so would injure them or others.

Practicing what we preach to our kids is a much more effective way of teaching godly principles than simply instructing or commanding that behavior from them. A humble apology from a responsible adult goes a long way toward teaching humility and proves to youth that God does indeed give another chance.

We give our children a valuable gift when we refuse to be seen as perfect or without blemish. Because of our God-given authority over children, we are tempted to present the perfect front. But children know better than anyone just how imperfect we are. What a blessing when we admit it, asking for forgiveness and seeking to right our wrongs.

10. Continued to take a personal inventory, and when we were wrong, promptly admitted it.

God is faithful in prompting us when we have been in the wrong. Practicing this step on our own could result in imagined wrongs that we make truly wrong through ill-advised confession. So we need to follow His promptings. Admitting our faults is hard, but the freedom of conscience and the ties of friendship thus gained are well worth the effort.

Steps 11 and 12

The final two steps bring us back once again to the only control we have over anything—the decisions we make about who will be in charge of our lives. By staying close to God through Bible study, prayer, and meditation, by listening for His promptings, by seeking His counsel throughout the day, we are able to receive from His hand and give to the children in our world.

11. Sought through prayer and meditation to improve our conscious contact with God as we understood Him, praying only for knowledge of His will for us and the power to carry that out.

12. Having had a spiritual awakening as the result of these steps, we tried to carry this message to others, and to practice these principles in all our affairs.

Grace and shame are opposite. Individuals in a grace-filled family, church, or group receive constant messages of love, acceptance, and worth so that they know that they are not alone to face life.

There are at least ten characteristics that describe for me the type of grace-filled relationships from which competent, creative, contented people emerge.

Truly Grace-filled Families, Churches, and Groups . . .

1. Affirm individuals out loud; everyone feels supported and nobody is marginalized or left out.

2. Are people-oriented rather than performance-oriented.

3. Clearly state their rules and expectations instead of leaving people to find out by breaking them.

4. Communicate clearly and honestly with each other instead of resorting to veiled or undefined messages.

5. Believe that God is the source of their strength and openly give Him credit for His working in their lives, believing that not to do so is idolatry.

6. Enjoy children instead of merely tolerating them until they grow up.

7. Teach individual responsibility and accountability through discipleship, not through punitive options.

8. Encourage the use of the mind for learning, not for defending or arguing.

9. Believe feelings to be valid and useful and not a sign of weakness.

10. Teach that it's OK for the outside of a person to match what is inside, so that people who feel empty need not act as if they are full.

---

1. See Eugene Peterson, *Like Dew Your Youth: Growing Up With Your Teenager* (Grand Rapids, Mich.: Eerdmans, 1998), 9, for the passages cited.

Gary Hopkins's comments:
We need relationships with each other, and we need a strong relationship with God. Jesus said it well: Our first and most important responsibility is to love God, and our second most important job is to love people (see Matthew 22:36-40). This means that we must learn how to help each other, learn not to enjoy the downfalls of others. Gossip in the church or community is no less serious than terrorism. Relationships and caring matter.

CHAPTER 33

The Man Who Might Have Been

by Kwame Ronnie Vanderhorst

Kwame Ronnie Vanderhorst is the outreach director and consultant for Prepare Our Youth (POY), Inc., a nonprofit organization headquartered in Washington, D.C., POY specializes in providing educational and counseling services to urban/suburban children and youth in need.

He is rich. Born into old money. His inheritance is great—his trust fund runs into seven figures. He attends a private school. He's the preppy, Joe College type. Everything has to be perfect—his afro neatly trimmed, imported leather footwear, exquisite cologne. He is religious and attends church weekly. He also frequents his share of stuffy bourgeois gatherings, chatting about investments while munching on brie cheese and sipping expensive wine. He's highly educated, his credentials impeccable, and he's listed in *Who's Who* as one of the young men of his country most likely to succeed.

His home is stunning. His walls are replete with priceless paintings. Valuable carvings and opulent artifacts, bought during his travels abroad, accentuate the meticulous decor. Luxury surrounds him. Servants respond to his beckoning call. A harem of women vie for his affections. Yet he is unsatisfied!

He summons his chauffeur, and they drive through the crowded streets of the inner city, looking. These are not the crowds he's familiar with—those who frequent the operas and famous art galleries. This is another crowd: beggars, drunks, commercial sex workers, tired mothers, burdened fathers, and snotty-nosed children.

"There He is, Sam. Pull over." The young man gets out of his vehicle as his personal bodyguard pushes "the multitude" out of his path, until he stands directly in front of Yahshua Messiah. And maybe without even saying "Pardon me," he interrupts Yahshua and asks a question that has disturbed him to no end: "What must I do to inherit eternal life?"

I hope you caught the word *inherit*. Life had been served to him on a silver platter. He was in line to inherit his family's wealth and possessions—why not inherit eternal life too? Yet, with all his privileges, Yahshua knew how he really felt inside. His unarticulated yearning (like that of some of us) was, *Why do I feel so empty despite all I have accomplished and all I possess?*

Yahshua Messiah cut through the facade: "Go, sell all your possessions, and give the money to the poor. Then come and share the burden of My mission by following Me" (see Mark 10:21). The crowd stood silent with bated breath and Yahshua watched with deep interest as this young man weighed his options. His moment had arrived. It is possible that his destiny hung on his response and he didn't even know it.

Beneath the veneer of opulence and achievement was a young man torn between his possessions and his pain. *"Sell all?" That's preposterous!* He opted out. Scripture says, "He went away sorrowful." He walked slowly back to his vehicle, where Sam stood awaiting his command. He looked at Yahshua one last time, and then his vehicle began to wind its way through the crowded city streets and out onto the open road. This rich young man reviewed the encounter in his mind. Confronted with a God-sent opportunity to make a profound life change, he rejected it. I imagine that from that day forward, the glitter was gone from his gold. I call him The Man Who Might Have Been.

One Way to Give

Like that young man, we've all been given a choice. We've been endowed with the ability and opportunity to serve others. Service to others is an antidote to selfishness. You can tutor, mentor, counsel, lecture, train, volunteer, or just listen to a burdened soul.

There are youth in the sphere of your influence who need your wisdom and expertise. I suggest that you try mentoring. A mentor is an instructor. A mentor transfers knowledge and skills to a mentee. At

Prepare Our Youth (POY), we tell young people to find a mentor who is in the profession or vocation they have chosen. That way the youth can discover what they need to know to reach their goal. For example, youth who want to become photographers can learn much that is valuable from a mentor who is a photographer. They can learn about cameras, how to develop film in a darkroom, how to put together their photo portfolio, how to sell pictures they have taken, etc. By the time the mentee matriculates, they will have a solid foundation in photography.

My youngest daughter Shalisha wanted to be a veterinarian. We were blessed to have a veterinarian in our church. My wife and I asked Dr. Michael Blackwell if he would mentor Shalisha (she was six years old at that time). Besides volunteering in animal shelters, Shalisha worked in Dr. Blackwell's office. She learned about the business side of being a veterinarian, about giving shots, performing operations, grooming the animals, and so much more. At age sixteen, she decided to pursue another profession—neonatology. Fortunately, we had a pediatric surgeon in our church. We asked him to mentor her. Shalisha is now attending Oakwood College. She has settled on becoming an orthodontist—and guess what! We have a dentist who is mentoring her. My point is that you can do the same for a young person interested in your profession or vocation.

When you mentor in terms of your profession or vocation, you are in your comfort zone. You know the ins and outs. You not only have expertise, but you also know numerous resources that your mentee can avail himself or herself of—everything from periodicals to scholarships that are available for youth in your given profession or vocation. Plus, you are filling a need and alleviating some of your *lack* at the same time. Whatever your profession or vocation, you can find a young person who has a similar interest in your church or community. You will be amazed at the reception you will receive.

Patrick Thomas came to POY at age fourteen from the Washington, D.C., Mayor's Summer Youth Employment Program. My brother Stevan, who is the executive director, and I took Patrick under our wing. Pat, as we call him, learned some of the essentials in acquiring a good work ethic: coming to work on time, being willing to do more that what is asked of him, having a good attitude, doing what needs to be done without being told, asking questions, being accountable and responsible, and learning how his job fits into the "big picture" of the organization. At age thirty-five, Pat is doing well. He is married, a father, and a hard worker. He volunteers for POY occasionally. At our 21ˢᵗ Anniversary Banquet on October 13, 2002, Pat was one of our special honorees. We feel honored to have made a difference in Pat's life.

The term *role model* has become increasingly popular over the years. Although it has its place, young people need more than observation. They need the practical involvement of every adult in some way or other. Mentoring is just one of the ways to make a difference in the lives of youth. You can mentor one individual or a group of youth who want to do what you do. All it takes is a little time and a lot of commitment. Few things can compare to the joy you will receive from having a part in the success of a youth that you mentored. Just think, that youth might become your surgeon, accountant, mechanic, attorney, plumber, or banker one day!

The life-rejuvenating, spirit-enriching joy that comes from service to others stems from a conscious decision to "sell all" our selfishness, apathy, and procrastination for the sake of prudently bearing one another's burdens. It is then that our example is read and practiced by those who are younger. To resist or to remain impervious only exacerbates our emptiness. We too may end up as the man or woman who might have been. God forbid!

CHAPTER 34

Conclusions: A Vision? An Invasion?

by Myrna Tetz

You've almost finished reading the book—there's just this one more chapter. You agree that it was soooo exciting. And in many ways so simple. But so real. So like Christ. We can, for the love of Jesus, bring back the youth who have left us and keep the ones we have. We can minister to small children. We can be real.

There's more to it though. Are you ready for the honest-to-goodness truth? We—that's those of us who are out of our teens and twenties and maybe even thirties—can have the privilege (that's what it is) of joining this electrifying conspiracy to change our church into a loving, affirming, ministering place. And here's the truth: Jesus told us that there must be no limit to our goodness because His goodness knows no bounds (see Matt. 5:48). That He gives to us—health, time, money, energy, love for His children—*only* so that we can give to others. And that giving is the secret.

Wouldn't you like to belong to a congregation where every child and every young person is bombarded with hugs and eye contact and is asked about their favorite activity? Where there's lively interaction between Sabbath School and church as the adults smilingly greet everyone? Where the "Songs of Fellowship" or "Praise Time" or whatever your church calls it always includes a couple songs for the really young ones and the youth? Where, when it's time for the pastor and the entourage to enter (do we still do that?), the group includes a child or young person to present the Scripture reading, announce the hymn, or call for the offering—or all three? Where there's a dynamic children's story by trained storytellers with an activity sheet for each age group? Where the main prayer will mention, by name, several of the younger set—different ones each week? Where the preacher always includes a story just for them during the sermon time or uses them to illustrate a spiritual concept? If this *were* your church, you'd have an invasion!

All of us want our friends to be, more than anything else, real people. We aren't often impressed with those who put on airs, those who have never made a mistake, those who say one thing and do another. "Authenticity means our walk lines up with our talk," wrote Rob Cowles.[1] That's meaningful as you review what you've just finished reading by this group of authors who were chosen because of their commitment to our children and young people.

When I was working on this book, I mentally recounted individuals in my life who had impressed me with their realness. For instance, my mother. She was a combination of fun and high standards, of humor and expectations. She communicated her wishes for us without our really realizing what she was communicating.

Under the couch in the living room were toys and games for children who came to visit. While the adults were conversing, mother would be on the floor playing with the children. And if the conversation turned toward topics she didn't want children to hear, she had a knack for changing the subject. Always she had something in her purse to help a restless child during church—paper for making a boat or a chain, a handkerchief for creating two babies in a cradle, pencils, crayons. She taught in the children's Sabbath School until she was deemed too old.

Her grandchildren could tell about all the silly games she played with them, such as Tease the Cat and Poor Pussy. She played football, although she never knew the rules and the game always ended in fits of laughter at her antics. She watched hockey with them and observed that if every player were given one of those "black round things," they wouldn't have to fight over it.

Now, because we have a notebook filled with excerpts from her frequent letters to her daughters during our college years, we can relive the example that she lived. She was *real*.

Years ago I worked in the Vancouver, British Columbia, Central Seventh-day Adventist Church day-care center under the leadership of Connie Zubke-Lange, a young woman who had adopted many of the Montessori methods of childcare. The major thing I remember about this youthful person who was in charge of a couple dozen young children all day, every day, was that she never spoke to any of them unless she was on their eye level. You've already mentally pictured her on her knees or sprawled on the floor most of the day, haven't you? You're right. That's exactly how it was.

We could all adopt her methods—speak to children on their level. Can you imagine getting a warm and fuzzy feeling while talking to someone three times taller than you are? Now, I haven't always followed her example—that's for sure. But we can at least bend over to smile at those with whom we interact (let's hope that's quite a few) and who are much shorter than we are.

Connie was *real*.

More Real People

Cliff and Jean Dawson are members of the Brooklyn, Maryland, Seventh-day Adventist Church. It isn't a large church, but because of the ministry of this couple and others, both the children of members and friends of the children of members are attracted to the Sabbath School, the worship experience, the Vacation Bible School, and other programs.

Children gravitate to Cliff and Jean like iron filings to magnets. I've seen Cliff sitting in the middle of the fellowship hall before lunch surrounded by a group of five or six young boys. What are they doing? Just talking. And smiling. Others are in the kitchen with Jean, hands encased in hot pads, helping to fill the table with food.

They've taken the children on Saturday night to the Chuck E Cheese's pizza parlor to eat and play. The next weekend the children surround the Dawsons as they excitedly looked through the album of photos, remembering that week-ago Saturday night. These children always go back to their homes with very special memories of their adventures with adult Adventists who love them.

Cliff and Jean are *real.*

There's another person I know who has a way with kids, and although he's now a retired pastor, his devotion to the young has not waned. During sermons, he almost always tells a story that the children can enjoy (in addition to the regularly scheduled one), and he just might unexpectedly begin singing a children's chorus during his sermon as he motions for them to join him. Other times he may ask them to help him demonstrate some spiritual concept. Each Sabbath he speaks to as many children and young people individually as he can. Just recently a member expressed concern in a Sabbath School class that there was a long-haired young man sitting in his car playing loud, raucous music. This pastor left the class, went into the parking lot, and stayed with him lest someone else reprimand him.

This pastor is *real.*

It was Christmas time, and my husband and I were purchasing gifts for our grandchildren—at Zany Brany. While he paid for our purchases, I stood by the table where three young girls were wrapping the presents we had chosen. On the table was a jar for tips. When my husband finished paying, I pointed to the jar and he went back to the cashier to get change for a five-dollar bill. I expected that he'd press a dollar on top of the others that were already there, but that's not exactly how it went. He stood in front of the first girl, pulled a dollar from his hand, bowed slightly, and said, "This dollar's for you." The next one, "This dollar's for you." And the third.

That cost a few minutes of our time and an extra couple dollars. Worth it? Of course.

Yes, he's real.

Others minister differently, of course. Some involve children and young people in dramas for the worship service each week, others include children in a variety of aspects of the church service, others lead in unique ways in Sabbath School divisions or Pathfinders, and some parents include their children in the Communion service.

These people are real.

A book entitled *Look at Me,* written by Jennifer Egan, says that in our world "reality . . . has been fetishized into a style, a simulacrum of authenticity that appears to satisfy the viewer's genuine longing for it, but, in fact, leaves him empty. And the media responds to that emptiness with ever greater contortions of simulated reality."[2]

This image-culture life of ours presents a kind of request, a plea, a desire for recognition in a *real* way. Somehow, our churches must be involved in satisfying this desire in our young people. Recognizing the parameters of the world in which we live, our ministries must provide an arena for spiritual growth. Listed here are some suggestions for you to share with your church and conference that just might enhance this growth:

1. Based on the perspective on ministry to children and young people that reading this book has provided, give a report in your church (or publish a book review in your church newsletter) suggesting ways to minister more effectively. Then share the book with others.

2. Write to your conference president and youth director urging new directions in leadership both in communications (workshops, articles, presentations) and funding to enhance the ministry to children and youth in your conference and churches.

3. Encourage the participation of children and young people up front in events and programs (that's called training them), and feature their goals and accomplishments in the church bulletin and newsletter. Giving them the Christlike attention they deserve just might mean their immediate or eventual involvement in sharing the good news that we treasure.

4. Urge your conference leaders to bring on more youth pastors and youth leaders. This would be beneficial to the young men and women whom they employ as well as those whom these leaders influence.

5. Ask that events be scheduled that help adults relate better to the children and youth.

6. Write notes or verbally express appreciation to individuals who devote their time and expertise to ministries for children and youth locally and otherwise and to the young people who participate in church activities.

7. Encourage your church board to include children and young people in board membership and all church committees. Suggest that it's also

important to ask for and consider seriously their suggestions.

As adults we have the great privilege of enhancing every young person's image of themselves as children of God as we relate to them in realness. Understanding the environment in which we all exist and the way we're unwittingly influenced by it should help to initiate and prepare better ministry opportunities for all age groups.

Let's be *real*. Let's pray for a vision. Let's prepare for an invasion.

---

1. Rob Cowles, "Understanding the Times," *Vital Ministry,* May/June 1999, 60–63.
2. See <http://www.jenniferegan.com/books/look/book.html>.

Gary Hopkins's comments:

The power of influence can be positive or negative. Research shows that mentoring has an almost unbelievable power (see chapter 17). Take the research on the Big Brothers and Sisters of America: Mentored kids are 46 percent less likely to use drugs— 70 percent less likely to use drugs if they are from a minority race (see www.bbbsa.org).

Let's look in the mirror and face the problem and then next Sabbath walk right past the adult Sabbath School and get into the divisions. *You* will make a difference.

Appendices

"Train Up a Child"
—Resources for Children's Ministry

by Louise Driver

Louise Driver manages the children's ministries department of the Potomac Adventist Book Center.

Have you thought about your child's personality and interests lately? What makes him tick; what rings her bell? When working with kids—whether they be our own or others—we may continue doing something over and over and wonder why we never get the results we would like to see. The answer lies in the fact that each child learns differently. Praise the Lord, there are so many different materials available—books and videos/DVDs, cassette tapes and CDs, and hands-on products. You can find these materials in Adventist Book Centers (ABCs) as well as in other Christian bookstores.

Stephen Ross has said, "A book is decidedly a silent teacher and former of the mind and character. . . . A frequently overlooked or ofttimes neglected necessity in the proper training of our children is . . . providing in the home good Christian literature which will guide them to faith in the Lord Jesus Christ. [This literature can encourage] them to serve Him and obey His Word, and will teach them honesty, kindness, purity, self control, faithfulness, etc."

There are books for every level, interest, and age group: Bible stories, biographies, stories, books about Christian living. Some are fast-paced time benders, others include adventure and friendship stories. Seventh-day Adventist publishers have provided an abundance of Christian reading material for our children and young people. Reading to your children Bible-story classics such as Etta B. Degering's *My Bible Friends* establishes an important life-long bond between you and them as you make happy memories.

A young child's book should contain lots of four-color pictures to make the story attractive to the child. In fact, much of the story will be "told" by the pictures in the book. Remember, children begin to learn to "read" by talking about the pictures on each page. To them, the pictures *are* the story! Note the books by Paul Ricchiuti, Karen Nicola, and Jerry Thomas. Kay Kuzma's *The Kim, Kari, and Kevin Storybook* is also excellent.

As children grow older, series like the Shoebox Kids Bible Stories fits their vocabulary and interests well. For those who want more fantasy, C. S. Lewis's classic Narnia series is a good choice. And humor is good too. Books like *My Life as a Smashed Burrito* by Bill Myers fill that bill. Don't be afraid to let your kids laugh while learning the lessons of life. In fact, have them read the books to you so you can share a laugh together.

The Detective Zack series never seems to lose its appeal. And don't miss the books by Maylan Schurch, Charles Mills, and Sally Dillon. To promote wholesome life values, encourage your children to read *Margie Asks Why, Michael Asks Why,* and the War of the Ages series.

Kids particularly like animal stories. To satisfy this appetite, try the story of *Jet the Crow, Grandpa's Furry and Feathered Friends,* and the Julius series, which includes *Thor the Thunder Cat.* Storybooks about horses continue to thrill young readers, so look for Katy Pistole's Sonrise Farms trilogy.

Devotional books encourage children to stay in touch with their heavenly Father. The newer ones are tuned in to what kids actually do. Some have thirty days of devotional reading, others sixty or even ninety days' worth. Research finds that's about as long as kids keep their interest in something; they probably won't finish a whole year's worth of devotionals from one book.

Teens will find inspiration in biographies such as those about Ben Carson, Jose Rojas, and Steve Arrington. There's also a compilation of past *Insight* magazine stories, as well as D. C. Edmond's book about relationships and sex. For other possibilities for teenagers, look for books by Steve Case, Gary Swanson, and Karl Haffner.

Coloring, sticker, and puzzle books of various kinds enable kids to relate to the materials interactively. There are great word-search and hidden-picture books available to challenge them, some of which are for the individual while others are reproducible for teachers to use in the classroom setting.

For children who prefer listening to reading, many books today come with a CD they can play while looking at the book (see, e.g., *My Bible Friends*). This captures their interest and encourages them to put feeling into the story when they do the reading. You can obtain Bible stories on cassette tape too. For instance, the classic *Your Story Hour* series has the Bible stories as well as stories from history and true-to-life adventures. These stories appeal to all ages, as does *The Bible in Living Sound*. These dramatizations of Bible stories make the Bible come alive and fix the stories permanently in their minds.

We all learn Bible texts better when they are put to music. Check your ABC or other Christian bookstore for Twin Sister and Cedarmont Kids products and see what other resources of this kind they carry.

Today's video/DVD resources are also excellent and growing more numerous all the time. Some videos/DVDs are companions to books, like Max Lucado's *You Are Special*. The child who might not read the book can watch the video and not miss out on the great story. Bible stories are available as portrayed by human actors and in animated form. The Hanna-Barbara series called The Greatest Adventure is still one of the best and most popular of the latter. The Beginners Bible Story series was produced for younger children. There's a series on virtues that covers friendship, forgiveness, and other Christian virtues. Children can watch this series of twenty-six videos over and over by themselves or with family and friends. The more they watch, the more the message becomes a part of their belief system. Check out "Derek," the high adventure game on CD ROM, and the board game, "Bibleopoly," which plays like "Monopoly."

The Veggie Tales series has many character-building videos that are not only informative but also entertaining. And the Veggie Tale product line aims at reaching all the senses and learning styles. Take the newest Jonah line: For the reader there are numerous books. For the creative child who prefers "hands-on" learning there are toys, puzzles, and games. The visual learner can benefit from CD ROMs and videos/DVDs. And the auditory-oriented child can choose from the music options.

Make Sabbath a special day for your children by setting aside certain books, videos/DVDs, and music for that day only. This helps the children think of Sabbath as something special—a time for family and friends and learning more about God.

Parents and leaders of children's ministries can find many materials available to help them in their task. There are books about how to recruit volunteers and books on how to work with children at various ages, interests, and capabilities. You can find books of games; books on storytelling, puppet ministry, and crafts; books that contain object lessons; and many choices of Bible studies for different age groups.

Colorful felts for storytelling are still popular with kids, parents, and teachers. Creative children will want their own felts to use on a small felt board so they can tell the Bible stories over and over again. This is a great way to start developing children's ministry leaders!

Good videos/DVDs, music, books, and games all help children become better prepared for adult life. You cannot overestimate the value of spending time reading to your children and of assisting them to choose good media products. Only eternity will reveal the returns produced by the dedication of parents and teachers to this aspect of children's ministry.

Shopping at an Adventist Book Center in the spring and fall of the year and at camp meeting time gives parents an opportunity to provide for their children attractive, interesting, and inspiring reading material for the entire year. For a listing of some of the newest publications available, go to <www.adventistbookcenter.com>, <www.pacificpress.com>, or <www.rhpa.org>.

More Resources

WEB SITES

Seventh-day Adventist Church Web sites

General Conference:

www.adventist.org (link to Children's Ministry Department)

http://www.youth.gc.adventist.org (Youth Department)

North American Division:

www.childmin.com (Children's Ministries)

http://www.nadadventist.org/ym.htm (Youth Department)

Other Adventist Web sites

www.adventistyouth.org/news (*Giraffe News*)

www.family-friendlychurch.net

www.gracelink.net

www.adventistbookcenter.com

www.pacificpress.com/kids/index.php (Pacific Press® Publishing Association)

www.rhpa.org (Review and Herald Publishing Association)

www.adventsource.org

www.lasierra.edu/centers/hcym/

www.cfye.org

www.AYradio.org

www.WeCare.andrews.edu

www.Camporee.org

www.domesticmissiontrips.org

www.pieceofthepie.org

Other Web sites

www.grouppublishing.com
www.faithweaver.com
www.childrensministry.com
www.YouthSpecialties.com
www.BibleActivities.com
www.ChildrensMinistry.net
www.ChildrensMinistry.org
www.lillenasdrama.com
www.Storytellingforpastors.com

BOOKS

Cheasebro, Margaret. *Puppet Scripts by the Situation.* Nashville: Broadman & Holman Publishers, 1989.

Flinn, Lisa, and Younger, Barbara. *Hooray for Children's Church.* Nashville: Abingdon Press, 1995.

Holford, Karen. *100 Creative Prayer Ideas for Kids.* Nampa, Idaho: Pacific Press® Publishing Association, 2003.

Reimer, Kathy. *1001 Ways to Introduce Your Child to God.* Wheaton, Ill.: Tyndale House Publishers, 1992.

Reimer, Kathy. *1001 Ways to Help Your Child Walk With God.* Wheaton, Ill.: Tyndale House Publishers, 1994.

Roehlkepartain, Jolene. *101 Creative Worship Ideas for Children's Church.* Loveland, Colo.: Group Publishing Inc., 1995.

Schroeder, Philip D. *Children's Sermons: Using the Five Senses to Tell God's Story.* Nashville: Abingdon Press, 1997.

Schultz, Thom and Joani. *Why Nobody Learns Much of Anything at Church: And How to Fix It.* Loveland, Colo.: Group Publishing Inc., 1997.

The phone number of the Andrews University Center for Youth Evangelism is 1-800-YOUTH-2U.

AdventSource (5040 Prescott Ave, Lincoln, NE 68506; tel: 1-800-328-0525; <www.adventsource.org>) stocks the Children's Ministries Association brochure; *Children's Church: Responding to God's Love*—a set of fourteen lessons for children ages 5-10; and the *Children's Ministries Manual.*

Strategies for Relationships With Young People

The testimonies and advice listed below are real-life examples of what individuals are doing to make young people feel significant to the Seventh-day Adventist Church. As you read, pray that you'll know which, if any, of these ideas suit your situation. (Several of these items have been condensed. To see the full versions, go to www.adventistbookcenter.com/olink.tpl?sku=0816319987.)

Estera Stefanovich developed an extraordinary ministry for college students. When she and her husband, Ranko, moved to Canadian University College in 1996, she couldn't work because of immigration problems. One day her husband told her about a girl who was very lonely and asked that she speak to this girl; maybe, he said, "she needed a hug." When Estera had provided some encouragement, Ranko asked if she would talk to a certain boy who was having some trouble.

As Estera prayed for these students, an idea came to her mind. She listed the birthdays of all the students (four hundred of them) on a calendar. Then she made birthday cards, baked kiflica (a walnut-filled pastry), sneaked into the dormitories, and put the treats in front of the birthday student's door. "And then," she said, "I'd run."

Eventually, one student who received some kiflica on his birthday called his father and told him. This father and others he contacted made funding available, and the school hired Estera (by this time she had her work permit) to continue her ministry on campus.

"You know," said Estera, "no matter what school it is, the students are smiling. But I find, working with them, that under the smiles so deep inside is sadness. . . . Money, houses, these are nice things, but nothing compares to being able to make some changes in the lives of these young people." (For the full story, see Penny Estes Wheeler, "Estera Stefanovich," *Women of Spirit,* November/December 2000, 18–20.)

Certainly there are individuals in academy and college communities who could bring treats to the dormitories for lonely, discouraged students.

Eleanor Friesen from Williams Lake, British Columbia, shares her memories and ideas for children's and youth ministries:

As a child growing up in the little church at Lamming Mills, British Columbia, I felt totally accepted by the adults. I helped address envelopes in literature band, and no one said my writing was immature. I went along on afternoon outreach programs where my only contribution was to be there, and no one ever said I was a nuisance. I was given responsibility as I grew; I felt part of the congregation, and church became a place I wanted to be because it was a happy oasis from a rather troubled home life.

We must invite the children and youth into our homes to get to know them and make them a part of our lives. This frightens some people, who think you must have a large game room filled with electronic toys. We discovered, however, that young people just want to be together. We also found that having them in our home week after week gave us a good indication of who were troubled and sometimes even what the trouble was—essential information if we were to minister to them.

Last year I looked around our church and found one family with two young children who do not have a grandma living close by, so I've adopted them as my church grandchildren. Their parents know my identity, but the children do not, so often on Sabbath morning they receive a little gift bag with a surprise in it. Sometimes it is only a few stickers or a little picture or a small inexpensive toy or a book. I sign it "From your church granny." They love it and look forward to coming to church.

Terry Self, from the Bloomington, Indiana, church:

The youth ministry team is dedicated to providing quality programs that will keep the children and young people interested and involved—kids' church, youth church, and Pathfinders and Adventurers Clubs. Our youth team believes that our greatest focus in the church should be evangelism for our young people

Kids' church is held once a quarter like an intensive Vacation Bible School. Each program, arranged around a story in the Bible, is presented with props and acting out the narrative with the assistance of high-school and college students. They also help with the music and select one child in the audience as a prayer partner. Craft time and refreshments are also a part of the hour-long program.

For youth church, we focus on issues pertinent to young people. We correlate these issues with a story in the Bible—for example, we combined the topic of dating/relationships with the story of Samson and Delilah. We arrange for guest speakers whenever possible. We always schedule youth church during home leave weekends in order to reach the academy youth who are away at boarding academy. And we always include food—a food of their own choosing.

We developed lists of attending and missing young people. When we started compiling the lists, we cried over the names as we realized how many we had lost. Each week after church a small group from the youth team meets and prays over the lists of names. We share new names, answers to prayers, and contacts we have made that week. Then we commit ourselves individually to pray daily for those on the list.

We plan youth recreation nights. We send cards, letters, and invitations and make phone calls to keep in contact with our missing kids. Whenever we see any of these youth, we start a conversation and express an interest in them and what they are doing. But most of all we let them know how much we care about them and what they mean to us. The Lord has greatly blessed our efforts.

Marilyn Morgan, a retired academy principal and teacher from Bloomington, Indiana, provided the following suggestions for using young people to read the Scripture reading and announce a hymn:

Scripture-reading suggestions:

1. Recite a scripture from memory.

2. Use a group as a speech choir. (Psalm 24 works well.)

3. Have two people recite antiphonally. (Psalm 136 sounds great when done by two people.)

4. Have four people take turns reciting the Beatitudes; each in turn looks at the other three when he or she recites.

5. Illustrate a nature psalm (such as Psalm 104 or 147 or 148) with nature slides or PowerPoint.

6. Sing a scripture.

Hymn-announcing suggestions:

1. Tell about the circumstances in which the lyrics were composed.

2. Tell about the origins of the tune.

3. Link the hymn to the scripture on which it is based.

4. Link the hymn to the Sabbath School lesson or sermon or holiday.

5. If the hymn has special significance in the announcer's life, tell why.

6. Have the congregation sing the hymn to another tune.

And finally, a miscellany of testimonies and suggestions point us to other ways we can make a difference to our young people:

• Paul Lehmann, director of the Outward Pursuits program at Canadian University College in Alberta, Canada (www.caus.ca), shares the testimony of a student named Anthony: "The three days and two nights were ones that I thought would never end. They seem to be engraved in my mind forever. . . . I had experienced. I had learned. I had been with God. I was immersed and enthralled with His great book that teaches us to allow 'nature to speak for itself' and puts us into a better listening frame of mind for God to speak to us."

Paul says that he dreams of more opportunities with young people in the great outdoors.

• Jack Carsello, an elder of the Boulevard Seventh-day Adventist Church in Philadelphia remembers that when he was very young, his family attended the Vineland Seventh-day Adventist Church in New

Jersey. A woman there, Mabel Dennis, allowed him to play the piano for Sabbath School and later helped him to transition to the organ. He says, "Her encouragement and faith in my ability to serve the Lord in this way, along with strong reinforcement from my parents, secured forever my love for sacred music." Though for a while he left the church, he has returned. And now he mentors young people by including them in musical presentations in Sabbath School and church.

• A pastor's wife who chose to be anonymous calls our attention to the "frightening" difference between the financial support for the children's divisions in churches and at camp meetings and that of the guest speakers for the adults. The latter receive travel expenses, per diem, salary, lodging and other expenses, and maybe even an honorarium, while leaders of the children's division, who are responsible for three meetings a day, may or may not be given lodging and meals and a small stipend and just possibly a small budget for decorations, crafts, recreation, and other supplies. Maybe this is a case of the location of our "treasure" revealing where our hearts—or at least our priorities—are. This pastor's wife believes that trained personnel and financial help are essential for those who lead in children's ministries.

• And Susan Schwarz, director of children's ministry in the Central California Conference, points to the endless hours in praying, preparation, and participation in programs put in by leaders and teachers. She says they have the most important strategy—they say, "I love kids. The Lord has placed within my heart a desire to work with and lead *His* children to the kingdom!"

APPENDIX D

Youth Survey

If you want to know how your youth feel about your church and your youth ministry and what topics they need help with, try this survey, developed by Mike Jones. At one time editor of Insight *magazine, he's now director of reclaiming ministries for* The Voice of Prophecy. *For youth responses to this questionnaire, see www.adventistbookcenter.com/ olink.tpl?sku=0816319987.*

1. Sex. (Circle one) M or F.

2. Age _____

3. How often do you attend church?
a. weekly
b. 2-3 times a month

c. once a month
d. _____

4. How much time do you spend in an average day in prayer, Bible study, or other devotional reading?
a. None
b. Up to 5 minutes
c. 5 to 10 minutes
d. 10 to 15 minutes

e. 20 to 30 minutes
f. 30 to 60 minutes
g. One hour or more

5. What do you like most and least about the church you attend?
Like most: _____

_____

Like least: _____

_____

6. On a 1-5 scale with 1 meaning Extremely Poorly and 5 meaning Extremely Well, indicate the extent to which the church you attend meets your spiritual needs.

7. If conversion means that one's life is 100 percent surrendered to Jesus Christ, do you feel that you are converted?   a. Yes   b. No.

8. In a sentence or two indicate your understanding of grace or note any questions you may have about this subject.

9. Please use numbers to indicate the top five issues in order of importance that you are facing in your life today. Write in any not included in the list that follows.

_____Conflicts with parents

_____ Issues with dating

_____Lifestyle issues (movies, jewelry, dress codes, dancing, other)

_____ Questions about what to do with your life, career choice, etc.

_____ Relevance of church, church attendance, need for baptism, etc.

_____ Double standards at home or in church

_____ How to know God personally

_____ How to know you're going to heaven
_____ Questions about Ellen White
_____ Issues with guilt and forgiveness
_____ Bulimia or anorexia
_____ Questions about values, what to believe, etc.
_____ Issues with pornography
_____ Issues about sex
_____ Insecurity and jealousy issues
_____ Thinking wrong thoughts and what to do about it
_____ How to know what's right and what's wrong
_____ How to overcome or cope with (you name it)

10. Note any issue or problem you are dealing with for which you would like to get some answers.

11. What nonphysical characteristic of yours would you like to change?

If you enjoyed this book, you'll enjoy this one as well:

It Takes A Church
Gary L. Hopkins and Joyce W. Hopp.

What role does the church family at large have in saving our young people? Gary Hopkins and Joyce Hopp provide a practical and potentially revolutionary "every-member's guide" to keeping young people safe and saved. Learn how to:

- Develop social support through a network of people who care.
- Open the doors of communication to talk about sex and values.
- Mentor our young people through strong, enduring relationships with adults.
- Recognize religion and spirituality as a powerful influence in protecting youth and preventing risky behaviors, and more!

Saving a child is every church member's business.

0-8163-1904-9. Paperback. US$8.99, Can$13.49.

Order from your ABC by calling **1-800-765-6955**, or get online and shop our virtual store at **<www.AdventistBookCenter.com>**.
- Read a chapter from your favorite book
- Order online
- Sign up for email notices on new products